27 R
ST

A Childhood in WW2 Glasgow

ROBERT CHESSAR

Grosvenor House
Publishing Limited

This book is published by
Grosvenor House Publishing Ltd
Link House
140 The Broadway, Tolworth, Surrey, KT6 7HT.
www.grosvenorhousepublishing.co.uk

A CIP record for this book
is available from the British Library

ISBN 978-1-78623-489-6

To my wife, Jane

Without whose hard work this would never
have been published

To my sister, Hetty

Without whose encouragement it would never
have been written

Contents

Introduction

It's December, 1942. Robert is 11 months old. His mother, Wee Jeanie, has news that his father, Driver John Chessar, has been killed in action fighting with Montgomery in Africa. She vows to her eldest daughter, twelve-year-old Hetty, that she will never tell Robert he had a father. His other sister, Jean, reacts badly to the sad news, and fights continually. Hetty takes the senior role in looking after the family. Without his father's income, the boy is destined to grow up in the dereliction and poverty of the Glasgow slums. His older brother, John, protects him from other kids. Jeanie's mother, brothers, and sisters want young John and Jean to be taken away from her to be raised elsewhere. Wee Jeanie defies them. She will raise her kids on her own…or die trying!

Robert's first conscious memory of the world is a faint recollection. He is nearly four years old and is sitting on a flat, smooth piece of concrete in the backcourt of the tenement. It is a sunny day. Two wee lasses, chattering like sparrows, are with him, playing with bits of wood and pieces of broken coloured glass found lying around. He is warm in the sun and blissfully happy with his sense of utter security in his family group. His experiences through the next eight years will alter that during traumatic, challenging, and character-forming adventures. Slum dwelling fosters defiance to feelings of being deprived. All he yearns for is to have enough money someday to buy a bicycle, a fur coat for

Wee Jeanie…and he would like to have a daddy. He discerns he has little chance to get any of these, but still hopes.

This is an account of his many adventures in the Cowcaddens area of Glasgow. His awareness of the difference between right and wrong is well ingrained. That doesn't mean he always acts in the right way. When he errs, the sound of blood rushing through his veins assaults his ears like an alarm, warning him to stop; or at least, be very careful not to get caught! He is constantly on the lookout for 'Joak Dan', the bad man who Wee Jeanie said would hurt him if he goes to places he is not meant to. Amongst his encounters with bullies, psychopathic idiots, and paedophiles, it is evident that he meets Joak Dan many times.

There is humour, drama, and a little pathos in Robert's interaction with the people around him in all their pride and squalor: the drunken old lady lying dead in a close; the very poor in spirit who gave up on morals and dignity to make ends meet; strong family bonds at times of crisis; adventures in dangerous places. There is poignancy as well in his coming of age experiences with both sexes. These are the memories of a boy doing his best to survive the trials of his childhood in the tenements of Glasgow.

But just before his twelfth birthday, he is catapulted into a perplexing and formidable world – a military boarding school in Perthshire. Suddenly his life changes from utter freedom to a regime of constraint and discipline. There he spends his teenage years coming to despise his once proud and humble beginnings. On leaving that place, aged eighteen, he is forced to return to the squalor of the slum tenements where he was born. In a place like this, what are his prospects of finding a career? Can he ever escape the dereliction of **27 Raglan Street**?

PROLOGUE: 1962

Robert was delighted. At long last, his house was to be demolished!

He was nineteen. Many years had elapsed since he ran about the Cowcaddens as a youngster with the 'arse hanging out of his trousers'. His life had changed dramatically during those eight years; six were spent in a military boarding school in Perthshire. His Glasgow slang had disappeared. He had walked back from his office to the same dirty old tenement in Raglan Street. His mother and older brother, John, were sitting in the kitchen. Jeanie greeted him with good news.

"We've had a letter saying Raglan Street's to be flattened. They're giving us a new house."

Robert punched the air, yelling, "Oh! You beauty!"

"We'll need to go down to the Corporation, Robert, to find out where they're going to send us and what kind of house they'll give us."

"A house with a bath, and hot water, and a kitchenette. At long last! A new house."

John was quick to quell his young brother's enthusiasm.

"Take it easy, Robert. We'll need tae wait and see what Mammy's being offered. They might send us tae Pollok or Castlemilk, or even worse, Drumchapel! Might even be just another tenement!"

"John's right, son. We'll need to wait. I hope we get something better than this. I couldnae stay in another tenement, and I don't fancy Drumchapel."

"I don't fancy *any* of those housing schemes," said Robert.

Robert's initial joy subsided. He took a seat by the fireside. They all fell silent, thinking their own versions of what lay in store for them. Their mother was now feeling less optimistic. Doubts were setting in. There had been so many disappointments in her life; she was mentally preparing herself for another one tomorrow. She hoped for a nice wee two-bedroom house, with a proper kitchen and the luxury of a bathroom and hot running water. All her life she had lived in tenements with single sinks and cold taps. Her last house was on the ground floor. They had to share a toilet in the back close with their next-door neighbours. It was in that house she had been left all on her own to bring up four kids: two girls and two boys, Robert being the youngest. This present house was three storeys up and had an inside toilet. *But tomorrow, surely to Christ! Things are bound get better?* thought Jeanie.

Next day the trio presented their letter at the imposing counter of the mighty Glasgow Corporation Housing Department. They were instructed by a stern-looking female public servant to "*wait over there!*" while their papers were found. They settled themselves on one of the wooden benches to await their next summons. Robert turned to his mother and joked,

"That woman looked like she was the model for the face on a Russian postage stamp!"

"Shhh!" whispered Jeanie with a smile. "She'll hear you."

The housing office was a depressing place. The brass door handles were polished smooth by years of use by people coming and going to pay their rent, beg for a house, plead for more time to pay, beg for a reduction in their payments, or some other clemency. The brass plates on the bottom of the doors were scuffed and dented by untold numbers of kicks from careless shoes. When the time came to be told their housing allocation, the *Russian postage stamp* called out, "Missus Jane Chessar!" They were the only ones there. They rose as one and approached the desk.

"You are going to Castlemilk. Here is the address. Go and get the keys from the end window and come back within five days to tell us if the house is suitable!"

"No!" said Robert.

"What!" said the postage stamp.

"Naw!" said John. "We're no' going tae Castlemilk, missus!"

"But you have to go there! There is no other option." She said this with an air of finality and a face drawn into a stare that threatened to take the very varnish from the counter. Her nose crinkled. Could she smell they were from the slums?

Robert leaned forward. "Then send my mother to Castlemilk, but you will be breaking up a family. Neither my brother nor me will go there! We'll be staying at 27 Raglan Street!"

"But Raglan Street is to come down!" was her final desperate gambit.

"Well, that's too bad! We'll both die in it and it will be your fault!"

The postage stamp swayed backwards with an expression of disbelief. She turned away, mumbling that her supervisor would deal with them.

John smiled. "No' bad, kid! When did you learn that?"

"Just now!" responded the boy.

Robert relished the power of his words. He was feeling, not for the first time, the bitter taste of being treated like a second-class citizen, a thing to be disposed of. That had happened many times in his life. Not now, though. He would not stand for that now. Not at nineteen. He was becoming a fighter, like his mother. The '*stamp*' returned with another female. They heard her say, *Is that them? Leave them to me*. Drawing herself up to a fully inflated chest pose, like a George Square pigeon, she stared at Jeanie and her boys and then marched towards them.

"Missus Chessar, you are to go to Castlemilk. Let us know whether or not you wish to take the house we are offering. Is this quite clear?"

Jeanie was used to standing up for herself. This attempt at coercion was a direct challenge. She relished direct challenges. Like a lioness protecting her cubs, she raised herself up, widened her shoulders, took a deep breath, and with control and dignity, spoke quietly and deliberately.

"Missus! I will do what is best for my boys. They don't want to go to Castlemilk so I won't waste your time by taking the keys. You can take it from me that the house is not suitable. Can we now get down to finding somewhere that my two boys *will* find suitable?"

"Hmmmph!" gurgled *the pigeon*. "You can't lay down the law here, Missus Chessar! We are trying to get houses for a lot of other people and we are very busy. So, you will have to take it or leave it, I'm afraid. You are not a special case!"

Jeanie was not to be put off. She would make this woman aware just how special *were* her boys. She had always fought for everything. At every turn there had been people who thought it was their job to make life as difficult as possible for Jeanie. She had battled with McAllister, the factor, and won; the rent was not raised. The coalman, Willie Blair, tried to do her for the coal money; that big man had failed. Before the war she fought with the coalmine gaffer, Joe Darroch, for the right wages for her man's double shift. And she won that as well. This lady of the Corporation was not going to win either. Not now! Not ever! Not when this was the best chance of a better future for her weans. Jeanie's dander was up. She spoke.

"Oh! But that's where you are wrong, madam. I don't know your name, but you certainly know mine. It's my married name. My late husband died nineteen years ago fighting for you in the war. That makes me a special case. That also makes my sons special. I raised these two boys and two girls, single-handed, with no money to spend on a fancy house. That is why I live in Raglan Street. If you are to knock down my *perfectly good house,* then you'd better find me a *perfectly good house* to replace it. Otherwise, I will die in Raglan Street with my two sons!"

The pigeon stared at Jeanie for some seconds. The air of superiority gradually subsided. In those few moments listening to Jeanie, her face changed from stern and uncaring to mild and forgiving, and then to a look of growing admiration. She seemed impressed by this woman's determination. Jeanie's dignified statement appeared to have struck a chord with her. She looked bewildered, perhaps now realising these folk were not just numbers on her list, but real people.

Jeanie noticed this slow transformation. *Had she made a good impression? Would her speech change things in her favour? You never knew with people in authority.* Jeanie felt, however, that something good was about to happen. The woman reached over the counter and touched Jeanie's hand.

"Missus Chessar," she whispered, "I must apologise to you. We see many people here who are not like you. I feel for you, for the loss of your man in the war, and I can sense the quality in you and your boys. Let *me* see if I can locate a place that you *will* find acceptable. Can I ask you please to wait for a little while longer? I will come back to you as soon as I can?"

"Certainly," Jeanie answered with a smile. She turned to resume her seat, escorted by her admiring sons.

Robert spoke first. "Wow! Mum, I didn't know you could talk like that. You're a hero!"

John corrected him. "Naw! Ma's a heroine."

"I'm not a hero," scolded their mother. "I just don't let folk get the better of me without putting up a fight. You two already know how to stand up for yourselves. Bullies are cowards and usually back down. If not, then you can at least get a hit at them before you get a doing," she said while giggling. "I stood up to that lassie without losing my temper. I got her respect and her sympathy. So now she is on my side."

The supervisor returned and called them over. She was smiling for the first time. *This looks good,* thought Jeanie.

"Missus Chessar, I have a very nice flat for you and the boys in the west of Glasgow on the Boulevard. It's newly-built and I am confident that you will accept it. It's two bedrooms, bathroom, lounge, kitchen, and central heating. I am sure you will be happy with it. Will you want to go and look at it?"

Jeanie returned her smile. "I think from what you said, it will do very nicely. Thank you. Please can I have the keys?"

That evening, they took the bus to Blairdardie, located the house, and went in.

"Oh, my! Isn't this just great, boys? We'll need more furniture to fill this house."

They walked through all the rooms and decided who would sleep where and how the furniture would be laid out. Jeanie, for the first time in a long time, was truly happy. She would have a room of her own, with a dressing table and all those other things she never had before. She would have a bedroom door to shut. Never again would she have to go down to the public washhouse for a bath. This house had all the luxury she could wish for. The tears came. John put his arm round her. Robert wanted to do that, but simply offered words of comfort. Jeanie spoke through her sobs of joy,

"Oh, I am so happy. This is better than I dreamed it would be. We will all be happy in this house. I will not miss Raglan Street one bit. Not now."

"Neither will me or John, Mum!" said her youngest, biting back his emotion.

A few nights later, Robert was sitting in the old house in front of the coal fire. He was on his own, wondering whether he *would* in fact *miss* the place where he had been raised. It dawned on him that very soon this old house would no longer exist. He felt that he was beginning to miss it before he had even left it. Raglan Street and everything connected with his early life would disappear. Contact with memories of his childhood would be lost forever. He was only weeks away from losing his roots!

He went down the stairs to the back close. Surveying the dereliction of the backcourt, memories from his past filtered into his mind. It was here that his character had been formed. All his childhood experiences had been here. The friendships he had forged and all the scenes of his life had been enacted in this dirty, derelict environment. He stared at a small patch of smooth concrete. This covered a repair to a piece of underground drainpipe. He recalled an image of himself as a four-year-old in shorts, hunkered down on that smooth patch, playing with some sticks and bits of glass. Two wee girls were with him, chattering like sparrows and laughing. His knees were warm in the sunshine. The trio was heedless of the neglected state of the backcourt. They were contented. Other memories from his childhood and many more of him growing up had formed a queue in his mind. He was lost in thoughts of adventures with his friends and troubles with his foes. A strong tap on the shoulder jolted him out of his pleasant reverie. It was John.

"Robert! Whit are you daen, standing here in the cauld, all on your own? Are you no' coming up tae the house?"

"Yes, I'm just coming up. I've been thinking about our life here, John. Maybe it would make a good story."

"Come on then. You can tell me about it goin' up the stairs, eh?"

"Right! It would start like this, John. *A long time ago I was happy.*"

"Is that right?"

"Yeah."

"Sounds like a good place tae start. Are you still happy?"

"Oh yeah, but I'm a bit sad as well. Remember when we were kids here, playing in the backcourts, the street and all the other places? The good and bad things we did for fun? The adventures we had?"

"Yeah! Ah do. It's been some place to be brought up!" laughed John.

"I agree. I think it would be good to write down these adventures before they are all forgotten and Raglan Street disappears."

"Aye, but who'll write it? Are you clever enough tae do that, Robert?"

"Don't know, but I'm thinking somebody should! Maybe it's up to me, since it's my idea."

They continued in silence up the last flight. Jeanie would be back soon from the dancing. In the house, Robert spoke again.

"John, do you remember Mum telling us recently the story about the telegram from the King saying that Daddy had been killed in the war?"

"Aye, Robert. She said it came at Christmas time, when we were jist weans. You wirnae even a year old, and ah was nearly five. It must have been terrible for Mammy. What made you think about that, Robert?"

"Well, John, that's where I'm going to start my story... December 1942."

ONE
December 1942

The telegram

Two days after Christmas, Jeanie Chessar's scream was loud and mournful, like a wolf that has lost its mate. She crumpled the piece of paper in her small fist, holding it away from her, trying to make the bad news disappear. As she rocked from side to side on her armchair beside the unlit coal fire, her other hand clawed at her hair as if, with physical pain, to overcome her trauma. Her wail subsided to a moan of hopeless anguish. Her young daughter, not knowing the reason for these tortured sounds, dropped to her knees and reached out her thin arms to try to comfort her grieving mother.

"Mammy! Don't cry! What's wrong? Tell me what's wrong?"

"Oh Hetty! Your daddy's dead!" she shouted, tears blinding her. "He's dead! Oh God! What am I to do?"

The youngster stared at her. She tried to understand how her father could be dead. Jeanie's harsh delivery of this awful news frightened her. All she could do was to yell back in defiance, "He can't be dead. Not my daddy. It's not true?"

1

"We regret to inform you that Driver John Chessar No T/280225 of the Royal Army Service Corps was killed in action on the 24th December 1942."

The Queen and I offer you our heartfelt sympathy in your great sorrow.

We pray that your country's gratitude for a life so nobly given in its service may bring you some measure of consolation."
George R VI"

Her mother thrust the telegram at her. It was blunt and to the point.

"The King says your daddy's life was nobly given!" Jeanie sobbed.

Hetty pleaded with her, hoping that the news was a mistake…that this was just a bad dream. She would wake up and everything would be all right.

"He isnae dead. It's somebody else, Mammy. Tell me it isnae him?"

"Ah canny. It says he's been killed in action. The King says 'consolation'. Well, it isnae! Jesus Christ! We've just had Christmas. Whit does the King know? It's no consolation we need. That'll no put food on the table or coal in the bunker."

Hetty laid her head in her mother's lap, sobbing the tears of a desolate twelve-year-old. Jeanie tried to console her, holding her tight, swaying back and forth trying to contain the aching hurt. She thought of her other kids: Jean was eight and at school; five-year-old John ready to go to primary, and Robert not yet a year old.

Jeanie shuddered, thinking how she would get by without her man. On his last leave from the army in June, he had been so proud to hold his baby son, Robert. Then he was off to Africa to fight, *'for his family's future'*. That was six months ago. Now their future was a lot less certain. The telegram lay crumpled on the well-worn wax cloth on her kitchen floor. The pounding in her head was receding. The wailing had stopped. She raised her daughter's head from her lap, cradling it carefully in her small hands. She looked into the child's sore red eyes and gave a sigh of resignation, gradually coming to terms with the reality of the news. She had to be strong and regain her self-control. Being active would dull the pain. She decided what to do; the news must be shared with her family. *Surely I'll get some help from them.* She spoke softly to her daughter,

"Right, Hetty. We'd better start getting things done. We'll go round and tell your Granny Campbell what has happened. She'll know what to do. Run out to the street and bring in Jean and John. I'll get the baby ready."

Her daughter stood up tall and straight, and wiped her eyes with the backs of her hands. She understood the abrupt decision her mother had made and she respected it. This was the way you got things done…head-on…get on with it. Not for the first time, she was witnessing the steely character of her diminutive mother. She was known as Wee Jeanie, but she was a fighter. She would need to be tough in the years ahead if she was to raise her children single-handed.

Knowing that Hetty would be gone for a while, Jeanie went through to the room and sat on her bed. From the chest of drawers, she took out her husband's soft bunnet. It had only been six months ago that he had worn it on his embarkation leave. They had gone to the Picture House in Sauchiehall Street. She lifted it to her face and closed her eyes. *Oh, John!* She sighed. *Oh, my poor man.* The scent of his hair

3

cream was still strong with the memory of that night; their last together. They had dreamed of the end of the war. Their future would be so good. The children would be better educated than them and get good jobs. They would grow old together, and have many grandchildren.

The realisation that these dreams were shattered was too much to contain. Wee Jeanie sobbed. Her tears were absorbed into John's hat. She held it to her chest as if it was him. *The man whose body I'll never hold again.* Shivering at the thought, she got hold of herself. *Right, John. You're away now. I'll put away your hat with these tears and I'll no cry again till these kids are grown up.* It was returned to the bottom of the drawer. She closed it. A long chapter in her life had ended.

She got up, went back into the kitchen, and stood at the window of her ground-floor tenement house to look out on the backcourts. The middens overflowed with rubbish. The battered metal dustbins had not been emptied in the last two weeks. Tarmac on the ground was pitted with holes, filled with dirty water. Broken glass from smashed beer and milk bottles was everywhere; trampled over many years to tiny pieces. An occasional shaft of sunlight fought its way through the dull December sky seeking the backcourts' soulless enclosure, making the glass particles sparkle like gems. The irony was lost on Jeanie as she surveyed this hopeless, colourless place. Cast-iron drainpipes hung precariously from flimsy supports on the outside walls of the tenements. Water seeped from loose joints, staining the roan-pipes with milky dishwater slime. The iron railings that used to separate the backcourts had been taken away to make guns for the war. This was her children's play area.

Jeanie looked down at her single black-iron sink with its tarnished brass cold-water tap. A chipped saucer, holding a cracked bar of Sunlight soap, lay on the worn wooden windowsill. Nothing around her was new. She had dared to dream of better than this. After the war was over, she would have had her man back earning good money as a coalminer.

Then she could have looked forward to a house with a bathroom, instead of having to share a lavvy in the back close with her neighbours. Her dream had been shattered by the dreadful news. The awareness of her inescapable, miserable poverty was hard to bear. Tears tried again to escape from her eyes. She remembered her vow and made no sound as she stifled the urge to sob. She lifted the soap and turned on the tap. The cold water lathered quickly. She bent and washed away the unwelcome tears. Her mind was crowded with doubts. She buried her face in the towel and swayed against the sink for support. She would never have gems! Her feelings of helplessness returned. *How am I to raise weans in a place like this? What chance will they have? How am I tae tell them they've no got a daddy? Who's going tae help us while there's a war on? I suppose it's all up to me. I'll just have tae get on with it. There must be many that are worse off than me. Ma maw's the only one I can turn tae. No use asking my mother-in-law for help. She's got her own problems.* Jeanie's husband was the older of the two Chessar sons. The younger one, Harry, was in the Royal Navy fighting the Germans in the North Sea.

Hetty would be back soon. Jeanie flung down the towel, rallied herself, and went to Robert's cot. The outside door opened. The girl came in with her two young charges. Hetty was a reliable lassie. Since her daddy had gone off to the war, she had willingly taken on many of the chores to help her mother. *Nevertheless,* thought Jeanie, *I will make sure she's appreciated for the sacrifices she's making.* On the other hand, Jeanie was not sure what the effects would be on young Jean. Her younger girl was headstrong and wilful. *I hope I don't have too much trouble with her. I'll try to be kind but firm and keep her under control.*

Wee John, nearly five, was not yet old enough to understand what had happened to his daddy. He had hardly known his father. The boy had been only three when his father joined up and went off to England for training. Young John had been a sickly baby. Jeanie recalled how he had nearly died at birth. The midwife had just left him on a table, thinking he was not going to make it. But he did. He was still a thin and weak-looking boy but Jeanie saw he had spirit and character. *He is such a happy boy. It'll break my heart to give him bad news, but he'll have to be told. I expect he will deal with it in his own quiet way.*

Robert slept peacefully, wrapped up and warm in his pram. With her family assembled, Jeanie set off on the short walk to her mother's house in Cedar Street. She knew there would be support and advice on how to tackle this awful change in her life.

Granny Campbell made a pot of tea, and fed milk and buttered scones to the children. Hetty was sent out to summon her aunties from Raglan Street. She returned with Katie, Lizzie, and Maggie. Once the condolences were given, Granny Campbell took control.

"We need to help Jeanie to get through this, so what can we do?"

6

Katie began, "I'm already giving some money to Jeanie since her man enlisted. I can give a bit more and help with the house after my work. Hetty will leave school in a year or so. I'll try to get her a job with me in Boots the Chemists."

Hetty listened without any change in her expression, but she was hurting inside. The sudden announcement that she was to leave school and find a job came as more bitter news. She was determined that nobody, least of all her grieving mother, would know that she was upset. She would do what was necessary for the family; just as her daddy had told her in his last letter: *Hetty, you mind and look after your mammy and the weans, especially Robert. I'll soon be home to take care of you all.*

Maggie had good wages coming in. Both her husband and one of her daughters worked in an engineering factory. She offered a little more money, and would continue to look after Robert to let Jeanie keep working in the Corporation of Glasgow school meals service. Lizzie had no way to give any money. Her man was not working. She had as many problems as Jeanie in trying to raise an even larger family. She had eight. She was a tough little woman who went out once a week to beg second-hand clothes and shoes from the posh houses in the West End of Glasgow. She lugged these back in a sheet over her shoulders. She resold the clothes and shoes to neighbours, earning a meagre income. Nevertheless, she offered to help her sister.

"When I've got a 'bundle', I'll give Jeanie first pick for the weans and no charge anything. But," she warned, "don't take too much, Jeanie. I've got tae live as well!"

Jeanie was grateful to accept these offers. She was a proud woman but, like them, she was practical. *From now on, charity begins at home.* She also had two brothers and another sister. They didn't live nearby. One brother was in Burma fighting the Japanese. Granny Campbell said she would find out in the New Year if those three were able to give some help.

Jeanie, meanwhile, went to the Soldiers and Sailors Charity to find out what they were able to do. As she was Roman Catholic, she also contacted the Parish Benevolent Fund people. This kept her mind on the problem of survival. The sorrow of losing her man resurfaced whenever she stopped to rest.

For other people, New Year revelries came and went. Jeanie had nothing to celebrate. Her grief had enclosed her whole family in an aura of sadness; not being aware of anything outside of their emptiness. The man in their lives was never coming back. This did not affect the baby. Jeanie thought, *How will I tell him about his daddy? He'll never know him. He won't feel anything about him when he grows up. We feel sorry but the baby feels nothing. There's no point in telling him.* She decided none of them would tell Robert that he had ever had a father, let alone that he had been killed in the war. In mid-January, just before Robert's first birthday, Jeanie was summoned to her mother's house. She arrived with her four children.

Her mother told her, "Bobby's away in Burma. Since his wife was evacuated out of the Clydebank blitz and moved to Helensburgh, she has her hands full looking after her new baby daughter and her elderly mother. I've not spoken to her, but I don't think she can help much, being so far away."

Jeanie said she didn't expect she would be in any position to help. Especially since Mary had been hurt in the bombing and had problems walking. "What about Charlie?"

"Charlie's working, but is finding it hard with three kids of his own. The boy with the cerebral palsy is taking a lot of their time and resources. His wife says she's very sorry about your news but is barely managing with what she's got without taking on the added burden of helping you out."

"I'm not surprised," said Jeanie. "At least mine are all healthy. I'll get by with what the rest are giving me. The 'parish' and the soldiers and sailors have promised to help as well. I've also had a visit from the army about a war widow's pension, so things are looking a bit better. What did Nellie say?"

"Well, she was very keen to help."

"Was she?" Jeanie was surprised at this.

"Yes, she said she would take young Jean off your hands. They would raise her as their own. Her man has the furniture business and it's bringing in good money. He's not keen, but Nellie says 'blood is thicker than water'. You could maybe ask the Chessars if one of them would take wee John off your hands. It's for you to decide, Jane," said her mother, calling her by her actual name.

"There's no decision to be made, Maw! These weans are mine. Ah'll raise them myself…or I'll die trying."

TWO
1945-46

The last couple of years were hard for Jeanie and Hetty. The help from her family allowed Jeanie to keep her children together. The house in Braco Street was made more secure. Her brother, Charlie, fitted slide bolts to the insides of the windows and put a mortice lock and a chain on the door that opened into the close. Hetty left school in March, as soon as she turned fourteen. Her auntie Katie, as promised, got her a job as a counter assistant in Boots the Chemist. She gave her mother all the money she earned. The youngster was proud of what she was doing to help, but she was still grieving sorely for her father. Jeanie had been awarded a war widow's pension of thirty shillings a week, including two shillings each for the baby Robert and wee John. Her wages and her family's charity kept them all fed and clothed. Their ground floor house was next to a busy pub. The noise through the wall and the smell of beer made it difficult and unpleasant for her and her children. She was heartily sick of chasing drunken men from her door for peeing up against the wall in the back close. At closing time, the noise of cursing and fighting in the street just outside her window made her determined to get another house. A house at least one stair up with an inside toilet would be a real luxury. Jeanie's sister, Katie, told her that the house above hers in Raglan Street was empty. If she was quick, she might have a chance to get it. Jeanie wasted no time in laying siege at the factor's office. Two days later, she was handed the keys for the house – three storeys up at number 27 Raglan Street.

Robert was barely two-and-a-half years old when they moved to their new house. He had no recollection of either having lived in Braco Street or that he had a father who died in the war. Until this point in his life he had simply existed within the security provided by his mother and his sister. He was unaware that there was a World War raging from before his birth and was still in progress. About a year later, on the 8th of May, 1945, Britain gained Victory in Europe (V.E. Day). Germany surrendered and that part of the war was over. Robert's earliest memory was on that day.

He was playing in the backcourt on a small patch of smooth concrete that covered a repair to a piece of underground drainpipe. He was wearing short trousers, hunkered down on that hot area, playing with some sticks and bits of glass. Two wee girls were with him, chattering like sparrows and laughing. His knees were warm in the sunshine. This trio was heedless of the neglected state of the backcourt. They were content. That was until they heard loud banging and hammering from the close. The wee lassies ran away. Robert went to investigate and stood watching in wonder as men ripped down the huge wooden beams from his close. The bombing from Germany was now over and so the timbers were no longer required to shore up the closes. The men hauled these out of all the closes and erected some at the top and some at the bottom of the street into two huge 'wigwam' shapes. People were packing paper, cardboard and wooden boxes into the space below. They all seemed happy, but it would be some time before Robert came to fully understand the reason for all of this strange activity and the party spirit in the street. People were singing and dancing. Music drifted out from open windows and a man played on his bagpipes. People in upstairs flats leaned out on their windowsills, shouting into the street, "We won the war! We won the war!" The child had no idea what a war was. He had his second earliest memory later that night in the street. This one was not so pleasing.

End of the world!

Later, just before dark, Hetty took her two little brothers down to the street. She held their hands firmly. Emerging from the close, they were all amazed to see the street lit up by flames from two huge fires. It was the wood from the closes. Flames leapt into the air as high as the buildings on either side. The timbers hissed and crackled above the roaring noise of the massive inferno. Millions of fiery sparks flew skywards. The intense heat, even from their far-off vantage point, was frightening. Eight-year-old John escaped from Hetty's grip and ran, leaping and shouting, towards the brightness. She yelled him to come back. Robert shut his eyes and hid, rigid with fear, behind his sister's skirt.

"Hetty! Is this the end o' the world?"
"No, Robert! It's the end of the *war*."

"Whit's the war, Hetty?"

"It's a bad thing that is now finished and everybody is happy,"

She said that to please the boy, but *she* was far from happy. She hated the Germans. They had killed her father, who was lying far away under the cold sands of Libya. *At least Robert will not have to bear this grief*, she thought. The fire and flames grew more intense. The heat was making windows crack and shatter, showering the street with shards of glass. John came racing back, his face beaming with excitement,

"Hetty! The whole o' Raglan Street's on fire. The windies are getting broke."

Folk were screaming. The smooth concrete surface of the street began to explode. Lumps of stone flew up into the air. People fled from the fire; it was getting out of control. No-one could stop it, even if they had wanted to. The war was over…so who cared if the place got damaged? At least it was them that did it and not Adolf Hitler. Fires like these were burning all over the city. There must have been more windows broken by these Glasgow folk in one night than by German bombers! The hellish scene in Raglan Street was to remain in Robert's mind. He would never forget this awful night.

"Hetty! Ah'm scared! Can we go up tae the house now?"

Hetty steered the two youngsters up the stairs to the safety of the house.

A kid for a tanner

A kind old Jewish man called Davy took a shine to Jeanie's amiable wee boy. Davy was a street trader with a big shed at the foot of the street, stuffed to the roof with rags and bric-a-brac. Often, when Jeanie went to her sister Maggie's house after work to pick up her son, Davy would admire the child's mop of blond hair.

"Missus Chessar, my dear." He always addressed her formally. "I want to buy this boy. I will take him off your hands for sixpence. It's a fair offer." And he would laugh and raise his black Homburg hat with a gentle bow.

"No thanks, Davy, he's no' for sale the day. Maybe next week, if things get any worse."

"Missus Chessar, my dear. Maybe next week the price will go down."

"It hasnae gone down since last week, Davy, but if you want him your price might need to be higher."

"Missus Chessar, my dear, you will ruin me. Goodbye, Robert, my dear."

"Cheerio, Davy."

Jeanie had a tight hold on his hand. The boy guessed that this barter for him was in fun. Even if it was not, he trusted in his mother to get a good price for him. A sixpence seemed to be quite a lot but maybe she could get a whole shilling. He liked this old man and had no fear of being taken over by him. He would still live in Raglan Street and be able to visit his mother every day if he got homesick. Davy would be like a daddy to him, since he had not yet got a daddy. This friendly association with the old ragman, however, led to an innocent act by Davy turning into a very serious situation. Robert's auntie Maggie had let her nephew go out to play on the pavement just below her first-floor window. That way she could occasionally keep an eye on him. So could old Davy, whose big shed was next to Maggie's close. It was the

4th of August, 1945. The Japanese had just surrendered and finished the war in the pacific (V.J. Day). Robert was three- and a- half years of age.

Old Davy stepped out of his store and, seeing the child, called to him, "Well, hello, Robert Chessar, my dear. How is my boy today?"

"Fine, Davy."

"Here is a gift for you. It's a shiny new farthing."

"Oh thanks, Davy."

"Did you know that you can get a chocolate ice-cream with a farthing, my dear?"

"Aye, Davy. I've been wae my brother tae the Italian ice cream shop in George's Road."

"Off you go, my dear. I'll see you later, eh?"

"Aye. Cheerio, Davy."

He trotted off to fetch his prize. The shop he wanted was on the left side of St George's Road, just round the corner from North Woodside Road. Robert had been taken there a number of times for ice cream. Sometimes he had sat down with John at a small round table to have a Macallum, or hot peas and vinegar. He was quite confident he would find the shop. All he had to do was to keep walking and looking and he would come to it. Without realising he had missed the shop, he kept on walking. He walked across the busy

St George's Cross junction and carried on till nearly at Charing Cross. He stopped abruptly at the point where the pavement took a dogleg to the right at the West End Ballroom. He had suddenly realised he was lost. In a blind panic at seeing no friendly face, he bawled the place down!

Meanwhile, his auntie Maggie was frantic. She had to find out where he had gone. She had no wish to be confronted by Jeanie when she came to pick him up after her work and found him missing. There would be blue murder if he came to any harm while in her care. She went to the phone on the police box in Lyon Street and told the sergeant on duty what had happened. An hour later, a constable came to her door and told her that the boy had been found a half-a-mile away. He was being kept safe in Camperdown Police Station. When she arrived and made herself known, they led her into the squad room where her errant nephew was perched across a wide windowsill. He was content to be basking in the sunshine while eating soft-bread rolls laden with butter and jam.

"Hello, Auntie Maggie!

"There he is, Missis Mathieson. Take him away before he eats all our pieces."

Maggie was happy to oblige. She got him back to the safety of her house before his mother arrived. When Robert told his auntie the reason he had walked off, she went down and told Davy what had happened. He was horrified. He promised not to do anything like that again.

"Missis Mathieson, my dear, please don't tell Missis Chessar."

"Sorry, Davy, but I will have to tell her."

"She will kill me, my dear!"

"No she willnae, the boy is back safe. Don't you worry, Davy. Jeanie likes you"

Jeanie arrived to a normal situation and a pot of tea in her sister's kitchen. She had no idea what had happened. Maggie waited till she was settled before letting her know. They talked on for a good while about this and that.

Reincarnation

As they spoke, Robert was busy playing on the floor with a toy his auntie had given him. The rule for children was that they should be seen and not heard. He was not paying any attention to his mother's conversation with his Auntie Maggie. That was until he heard a phrase that registered like a dart in his brain.

Jeanie said, "…when John died…"

She was, of course, referring to the boy's father. Robert wondered how this could be? The only 'John' he knew was his brother. With a child's logic, he thought he understood what Jeanie had meant. *My big brother, John, had somehow 'died' and had then come back to life again.* There was thus no need to interrupt the grown-ups to explain. It was simple. You died and then, when you had done that, you came back to life again. This thought gave him comfort. It meant you could do dangerous things and, if you died in the process, it didn't matter. It would not dawn on him, until many adventures later, that his mother was referring to his father, John, who died in the war, not his brother. He did not know that his father, John, had ever existed; thus he did not miss him. In his head, however, there was a notion that something *was* missing from his life. Everybody except him knew about his dad. The boy was treated with kid gloves because of it. This had its advantages. He was rarely chastised, treated with fondness, and spoiled by aunts and uncles. All of them were sorry for 'wee Bobby'. *How he must miss him,* they all thought. He was oblivious as to why he got this treatment but loved the attention.

His impression was that he was a very special kind of child. *Hadn't those men and women in the police station fed him like a little prince?* He sensed he could do no wrong. He asked and he got. He enjoyed being spoiled. He played on it, but even at this young age he was clever enough not to let this show.

Charity begins at home.

Jeanie was scraping by. Without a man in the house, of necessity she was firmly in charge. Her best help came from her teenage girl. Hetty took on a lot of the menial chores, as well as trying her best to coax the younger ones to be good, be clean and, most importantly, be quiet. Things were going along fairly well for them. It was in the weeks after the fall of the Japanese that surviving servicemen began to return from overseas. Maggie's boy, Bertie, was already home but would soon be shipped out with the paratroopers to the trouble in Palestine. Bill Murray, Lizzie's son, was home from the navy. Jeanie's brother, Bobby, had returned from Burma. *All in all, the end of this war is bound to bring hope for a better future for my kids and me. It's a shame John's not coming back, but we'll just get on with it. We'll manage fine with what we've got.*

She had the house to herself one day. The four of them were out – the boys playing with other boys, and the girls doing the same or chasing boys. There was a knock at the door. *Who can this be?* She got up and went to answer it. It was a stranger. A woman with a collecting can: a taped-up, dried milk tin with a label stuck to the front.

"Yes. What do you want?"

"We're collecting for the soldiers."

"What soldiers?"

"The soldiers returning from the war."

"Why are ye not collecting for the ones that *arnae* coming back?"

"Well, they don't need it, do they? They're dead."

"But their families – their wives, their children – they arnae dead. Are they?"

"What's that to do with you? We're just looking for some charity."

"Listen you to me, missis! I'll tell you what it's got to do with me! My man's one of the ones that's no coming back. In this house, charity begins at home. You've got my man's life and that's all the charity you'll get at this door. So, you can just take yourself and your collecting can, and bugger off!

Jeanie slammed the door and went to sit down by the fireplace. *What a bloody nerve*! She was fuming. It wasn't the first time that she lost her rag with people in Raglan Street and it wouldn't be the last. She retrieved John's bunnet from her private drawer, held it to her face, and whispered into it, "You've no need to worry, John. I can take care of your weans."

THREE
1947

Jeanie had done well in the last five years. With her own money from the school meals service, her war widow's pension, and wages from Hetty, she had managed to keep her family together, clothed and well fed. She felt safer and happier in the third-storey room and kitchen in Raglan Street. In the bedroom, Jean, John, and Robert slept together in the wide bed in the recess. Hetty slept with her mother in the double bed next to the fireplace. Things were much better here. Her neighbours kept themselves to themselves. This was a far cry from that dirty, rowdy close in Braco Street where she had to keep her windows closed and bolted day and night. It was still a struggle, but at last she was seeing improvements in her life.

There had, however, been a bit of trouble with Hetty. She had worked in Boots the Chemists with her Auntie Katie for over two years. A month or so ago, she told Jeanie that her shop manager touched her and she was embarrassed. Jeanie got hold of Katie, who took Hetty to the shop to confront the man. He, of course, denied everything. Katie believed Hetty. She resigned on the spot, taking her niece with her. She wrote a letter to the head office explaining why they had left. It worked out quite well for them. The manager was dismissed; Katie and Hetty got their jobs back. Three weeks later, Hetty got a new job as a typist for the William Collins Company, the big printing and publishing firm in Glasgow. Jeanie was delighted that her daughter was going up in the world, working in an office. This was a big change in Hetty's life; something to tell her family…but not her neighbours. Another big change was about to happen. Tomorrow, Robert was starting school.

School

Jeanie took him down to Grove Street Primary School for his first day. Jeanie's apron strings were now severed for the fourth and last time. Robert was a bit apprehensive, but he knew that his big brother, John, was already there, so it didn't bother him too much. His main concern was how he would deal with the new boys and lassies he was to meet. Jeanie was directed to the primary one classroom. She knocked on the door.

"Come in!" said a female voice.

"Hello, I'm Missis Chessar. This is my son, Robert."

"Hello, Missus Chessar. I am Miss Robertson. Robert, you sit here in the front beside John Carly. He'll be fine, Missus Chessar. You can come back for him at three-thirty. Thank you for bringing him in."

"Cheerio, son," said Jeanie as she left. He said nothing.

The teacher turned to the class, pointed to the new arrival and said, "Robert, please stand up."

He stood up.

"Tell us all your full name, Robert."

"Ah'm Robert Campbell Chessar."

"Say hello to the class, Robert."

He turned round. "Hello."

"Now, class, say hello to Robert." They chorused their welcome.

"Now. Robert is a very formal name. I think we might call you Bobby. Will that be all right?" She hoped he would be pleased with this affable form of his name. His stern rebuke took her by surprise.

"No, it willnae be all right. My name's Robert and that's what ah've tae be called."

She was impressed. Her new pupil was not afraid to stand up for himself.

"Oh my! Well, class. It seems his name is Robert. We will call him that and no other name. Do you all understand that?"

"Yes, Miss Robertson," came the chorus.

She smiled. "Now, *Robert,* you may sit down, and we can continue with our lesson."

Robert sat down to begin his first day at school. He was known from that day on as Robert. He was never called

Bobby, Bob, Bert, Bertie, Boaby, Robbie, Rabbie, Rob, Rab, or any other diminutive of his name. At least, not in his classroom!

Praise

He adjusted well to the new disciplines of school. He was pleasant to his teachers and enjoyed learning to read, write, and count. He was not the brightest in the class, but no dumb-head either. On Fridays a ceremony was enacted in the classroom. Some pupils went out to the front to be given a sweetie from a jar. This was the reward for having enough stars in their jotters for neatness, correct spelling, counting, and being attentive during the lessons. Robert wasn't too happy about never quite having enough stars to get out to the front. It always seemed to be the same boys and girls who got the sweeties. One Friday, after the predictable prize hand-out, Robert lingered in his seat while the class dispersed. He wanted the teacher to know his feelings but didn't know how to say so.

She saw him sitting deep in thought. "Robert, are you waiting for something?"

"Yes, Miss Robertson."

"Well. What is it?" said his teacher, coming over to him.

"Why do I no' get out tae the front on a Friday? It always seems to be other people."

The teacher was quite taken aback by the question. She thought for a few moments about this, in a quandary as to how to tackle the answer. She did not wish to offend her obviously troubled pupil.

She spoke in careful tones. "Robert. You get stars in your book when you have done well. The pupils who get the sweeties are those who have the most stars. Do you understand?"

"Yes, miss, but ah've got some stars in ma book but ah don't get out to the front for a clap from the rest."

"Oh! I see." He was not so much interested in getting sweets, just to be seen to have stars. "Robert, perhaps we can do something about that. Wait till next Friday and see what happens. I promise you will not be disappointed."

"Thanks, miss."

He turned to go. The room was now empty bar her and the boy. She called him back, held out the jar of sweeties to him and whispered, "It took courage to speak up the way you did, and that deserves a reward."

He took his very first sweetie. "Thanks, miss."

The next Friday, the teacher was true to her word. Those who normally won…won! But there was another presentation when the teacher said, "Now, class. All of you who got stars this week, stand up."

Most of them stood up. She knew that Robert had three.

"Now anyone who got three or more, come out to the front. Give them all a clap. I want big efforts next week from those with two or less. Now off you go!"

Robert was proud of his moment of fame. He felt comfortable in this new real place, gaining in confidence, not afraid to speak up for himself, and adept at manipulating grown-ups to get what he wanted. This aside, he had frequent thoughts of a different reality. A lot of his schoolmates had daddies. He had often wondered what it might be like if he had one. It would maybe make his mother happy to have one around to help in the house. It might even mean a bicycle for him? His mother might get the fur coat she was always talking about. He decided that having a daddy would be a good thing.

With growing confidence, he thought, *all ah have to do is ask, but ah'm only five; maybe Mammy will want tae wait till ah'm bigger?* He put the idea out of his mind, but the desire for a father was stronger than he thought.

Guardian angel?

The war was still a vivid memory for grown-ups, but Robert had no recollection of it apart from the frightening bonfire night. He was put to bed as usual by nine o'clock, to be well rested for school in the morning. The bed recess had a curtain to make it dark. Comforted by the sounds of his family's voices drifting through from the kitchen, he soon fell into his usual deep sleep. Normally he would sleep right through the night…but not that night. He sat up, fully awake, eyes wide open, facing the back wall of the recess. He was alone. *Jean and John must still be in the kitchen.* Something told him that he should get out from under the covers and crawl to the front of the bed. He could still hear the sounds from his family. He reached the edge of the bed, pushed the curtain to the side, and looked out into what should have been an empty room. Light from the street filtered through the curtains on the two sash windows, giving the room a soft moon-like glow. The bed where Hetty and his mother slept was diagonally opposite. He saw a soldier in khaki battle dress between him and his mother's bed.

The man was kneeling on one knee. His left hand held his rifle; its butt resting on the floor. His right hand held onto the wooden end of the bed. He was wearing a tin battle helmet. The face below the rim was young and smooth. The soldier was not facing Robert, but was looking straight ahead towards the windows. He was motionless and utterly silent. Any young boy might be excused for shouting with fright at seeing such an apparition that had no business being there. For some strange reason, Robert was not in the least bit alarmed by this presence. The effect of seeing this figure was remarkable. Robert felt comfortable and safe. Some sensation within his head told him that this soldier was keeping a watch over him.

He smiled and let go of the curtain, and returned to the comfort of his bed. Snuggling into his still warm blankets, he drifted back into his dreamless sleep. In the morning he didn't mention this to anyone. He seemed to understand that his experience was for him alone, and without any selfishness, he had no need to share it with anyone. His seeming dream had a kind of realness and he was not afraid of it. He was not sure whether he had been awake or sleeping, but he was reassured by it. No-one had yet told Robert of his father's death in the war the year he was born. All he knew and felt was that he was under the protection of some entity that had visited him, and him alone, that night. The 'visitation' that had taken place happened long after any soldiers had been on the streets with rifles and wearing tin helmets. The rational explanation for what he saw that night perhaps would be that he had a deeply sub-conscious desire to have a father, like his pals. Such a strong desire could, probably, manifest in an hallucination. Dream or not, Robert liked it and made up his mind to ask his mother to get him a father.

Next day he confronted her. "Mammy, when will we get a daddy?"

Jeanie was taken unawares by this out-of-the-blue direct question. She recalled her decision that to protect the boy, he should not be told of the tragic death of his daddy. She felt a pang of regret that he was innocently under the impression that he had never had a father, but it was not yet the time to tell him the truth. She wasn't sure when the right time might be, but she was not ready to do it soon, and certainly not there and then. She stuttered a quick response hoping it would keep the subject away for a while longer.

"Oh son, we'll get one when we have more money."

"How much does a daddy cost, mammy?"

"I don't know, son. We would need a bigger house, and that is very expensive.

"Why do we need another house?"

Jeanie was getting desperate. She was short of excuses, and decided to finish the conversation before she got too frustrated and blurted out the truth.

"Because he would have nowhere to sleep, son, and we'd need a bigger bed and everything. Now, I want you to go up to Peggy Clark's and get me half-a-stone of potatoes, there's a good boy."

She was relieved that he seemed to be satisfied with her abrupt reason and her diversionary tactics. He went to the shop as directed, still none the wiser. On the way, he mused on his mother's answer: *maybe Mammy disnae want a daddy in the hoose. Maybe we don't need one. I wish ah knew how some ae my pals have daddies. They're just as poor as us. Ah canny understand this.*

He spoke to his big brother but got nowhere. He didn't know anything either, he said. Robert thought he might ask his Auntie Katie, but decided against that. The other day she had given him a fright by speaking brusquely to him. He was not used to such treatment.

Church or chapel

Katie had to look after him the previous week, because Maggie was not available. This coincided with an obligation of Katie to go to church. She took her nephew with her, thinking he would be no trouble. St Joseph's Church in North Woodside Road was a magnificent building. The inside was spectacular. The only building he had been in that was like this was a cinema. Just before the service started, when all was very quiet, a small voice, clear and piercing, was heard to say, "When dae the pictures start, Auntie Katie?"

In seven brief words, he informed the congregation that he was a Protestant interloper, innocent of the purpose of this building. He was bewildered to see the folk nearby giving him looks. These turned to knowing smiles on seeing the fair-haired cherub being shaken briefly by his affronted auntie. Katie whispered harsh words into his ear. He was not sure why he was being chastised like that and sat back in a sulk. It would be some time yet before he came to understand some of the invisible social barriers erected by his elders.

FOUR
1948

Robert saw many soldiers in Glasgow after the war with Germany came to an end in 1945. Another war had just come to an end for Britain. People like Robert's cousin, Bertie Mathieson, policed the conflict between the Jewish settlers and the Arabs in Palestine. His Auntie Maggie's son was a paratrooper. When he came home, he took a great liking to his wee cousin. Robert spent a lot of time with Bertie and his soldier pals. He was often taken to the snooker hall at St George's Cross to watch them playing. For cheering them on he received many sweets and bottles of orange juice.

Up at his auntie's house with the gang of big strong soldiers, Robert asked, "Bertie, what's it like being a paratrooper?"

Bertie lifted him up to the pulley. "Kid on you're in the aeroplane. Hing on!"

"Ah'll fa', Bertie!"

"Naw ye'll no. Hing on tight."

"Ah'll hurt maself!"

"You're a' right."

"Bertie! Ma trousers are fallin' doon!"

"Naw they're no'. Haud on tight. When ye let go, bend your knees and roll tae the side."

"OK, Bertie."

"Let go! You'll no' hurt yourself."

The boy let go, bent his legs, and rolled easily on the floor. He stood up and pulled up his breeks, yelling, "Bertie! That was great. Was that as good as youse?"

"That was the best ah've ever seen, Robert. You'd make a rare paratrooper."

Although he had only fallen about three feet, he felt he was a real soldier like his big brave cousin and his pals. He loved being with these four big-hearted heroes and felt very safe and protected when he was with them, listening to their jokes and stories of their exploits.

When he was out playing in the street, Robert was mostly under the protection of his big brother, John, now ten years old. John had grown tougher during his time in primary school. He was a good fighter. He told his wee brother, "The best form of defence is attack." John had a reputation in Raglan Street. All Robert had to do was say he was John Chessar's wee brother... The usual response was, "Better leave him alone, he's Chessar's kid brother."

This tactic didn't always work, but did so on enough occasions to save him and build his confidence and cunning!

One thing scared him. Jeanie told him if he went to places he was not allowed, a bad man called *Joak Dan* would get him and do bad things to him. The warning was effective. He was vigilant and wary of meeting this scary person. He had no idea what he looked like, but the name 'Joak Dan' didn't sound like a joke. He promised his mammy he would be very careful. He knew he could relax his guard while out with his big brother. John guided him through some exciting and dangerous adventures. About some of these, Jeanie was unaware.

Jack's Mountain

Up at the Forth and Clyde Canal near the Pinkston Power Station, there was a hill called *Jack's Mountain*. The inside was scooped out like a volcano, a couple of hundred feet across. Access was gained by scrambling up the steep outside slope and slithering down the inside. The crater had a wide, smelly stagnant lake about two or three feet deep. This 'lake' was affectionately known as *The Stinky Ocean*. The place was strewn with rubbish, old oil drums, and sundry chemical wastes. The surface of the water was a patchwork of multi-coloured dyes. It was almost attractive... except for the smell.

The fetid liquid was a graveyard for cats and dogs. Unwanted kittens were disposed of in sacks thrown into the vile water, ensuring an unmerciful end. Racing dog owners were not prepared to feed a greyhound that wouldn't win! The reward for such a mutt losing at Firhill dog track was to end up dead in the canal, or even worse, in the putrid soup of the Stinky Ocean. The predominant stench from the place was like rotten eggs, mixed with those of paints and putrefying animals. Add to this cocktail, the smoke from fires lit by gangs of kids. By building fires, they at least helped to dispose of discarded furniture, linoleum, and sundry other detritus lying around. It was into this fantastic playground that kids drifted from the surrounding tenements to play. There was no guilt felt about increasing its destruction.

Robert would never have dared go there except with John. Boredom had occurred in Raglan Street. A shout went up, "Come on! Who's coming up tae play at Jack's Mountain?"

John and Robert became part of the hurriedly assembled gang. The adventure began at the top of Baird's Brae beside Oakbank Hospital, where both John and Robert had been born. They all ran along the canal past the warehouses towards Port Dundas. At the power station, they stood at the open doors watching men shovelling coal into boiler furnaces. This noisy, gloomy place, with its dirt and flames, was menacing. Seeing this scene for the first time, Robert was fascinated and nervous.

"Is this where the Devil lives, John?"

"Naw, Robert, this is a good fire."

"How is it a good fire?"

"Well, it gives men jobs, and heats up the canal tae keep the fish warm."

"So this isnae the 'bad fire' you go tae when you're bad?"

"Naw. When you're bad you go tae Hell and burn forever!"

"Is it hotter than this, John?"

"Oh aye. A hunner times hotter. You widnae want tae go there!"

"Ah'm frightened. Can we go somewhere else?"

"Aye. Wait tae ye see what's roon the corner!"

He was referring to the abattoir! Opposite the power station was a run-down brick building where they slaughtered horses. Loud bangs were heard coming from the building as the gang went past the open door. The older boys, although never having seen it, told the young ones that it was the slaughter-man in the back, killing animals with a gun. What they did see were horses hanging on hooks, being split down the middle, their insides gushing in a bloody mess onto the stone floor.

One boy said he felt sick. Others were fascinated by the apparent brutality of these butcher men. Ever inquisitive, Robert asked, "John, is there too many horses so they have tae kill them?"

"Aye. Could be, but ah don't really know why they do it. Mibby it's because everything is done wae motors and lorries noo. So then the horses don't have anything tae do."

"That's a shame."

"Aye, so it is. No much reward for working hard all their life, eh? Come on, let's get going."

The bunch moved on towards its final objective…*The Stinky Ocean*!

Robert was open-mouthed on the ridge of Jack's Mountain, staring for the first time down into the Stinky Ocean. He had already experienced enough strange sights, sounds, and smells on his journey to this foul destination. This one was the worst. His response was to turn and to start to go back the way he had come.

John stopped him. "Where are ye going, Robert?"

"I don't like this place, John!" the youngster whined, looking at the scene in the crater. "Ah think it's too dangerous and ah'm scared. Ah don't like that dirty water! It looks deep!"

"You'll be alright, Robert. It's not deep. Jist stay wae me. Come down tae the bottom and you'll see what it's like."

Joining hands, they made their way down the slope to the water's edge. A commotion of activity began. A fire was lit. Dry horsehair stuffing from an old armchair created a good blaze. Paint tins and cardboard boxes had the fire going well. Regular prodding with sticks made plumes of smoke and sparks. For the older connoisseurs of a good fire, all was right with the world. John watched out for Robert, and kept him a safe distance from the water and the fire. He also looked out for anyone getting too close to his wee brother. No-one would be allowed to harm his youngster. John was always ready to step in to halt any such approaches.

His first warning at any sign of encroachment on his kid was, "Hey, you! That's ma youngster! Leave him alone!"

At that, most people stepped back, well-aware of John's reputation. "Sorry, Chessar! Didnae know he was your youngster."

John's second warning was abrupt. "Well, he is! So fuck aff!"

Robert started to relax. He was sweating from the exertions of reaching this unholy destination; happy to stand beside the fire beside his bodyguard, feeling the heat drying his sweat and stinging his face. The place gradually took on a reassuring sense of security for him, with all the boys standing together, taking their turns to chuck more stuff onto the fire or to run for more burnable rubbish lying around. He wandered over a little closer to the lake to watch, wide-eyed, at two lads fetching in the bloated carcass of a greyhound. As it floated nearer, they began to throw stones at it, attempting to burst it open and hear it explode. A carefully aimed half brick did the job. The dog's body hissed for a second or two, filling the air around with the worst smell imaginable. But the little savages were not yet content. They continued their assault on the poor dead creature, hitting it with sticks until its yellow stomach contents and the rest of its intestines were being strewn around, amidst a wild extravaganza of crazy whoops from some and gurgles of disgust from others.

John went over and pulled his brother back to the fire. Then he noticed an ominous presence. A line of foreign troops appeared on the opposite ridge of the volcano. He sensed danger. He took Robert's hand and slowly steered him away from the fire. A few steps more and they were closer to their avenue of departure. Part-way up the slope. he heard the first verbal salvo from the enemy.

"Heh, youse!"

On this sudden and unexpected salutation, the gang demolishing the dead dog and those around the fire froze! In John's estimation, this amounted to a declaration of intent to attack. He and Robert were nearly at the top of the crater before the others had started to turn away. Their enemy became more confident and warlike.

With gathering bravado on seeing the early stages of a retreat, they shouted, "We're gonny kill youse! Wait there tae we come an' get yez!"

The attacking marauders had reached the bottom of the opposite slope. They began to skirt the lake. The Raglan Street crowd had by now established a safe flight-distance. They bawled back, "We're no waiting! Youse'll have tae catch us!"

They turned and ran for their lives up and over the ridge, catching up with John and Robert at the railway bridge. Their swift retreat, trotting in a pack back along the canal, ended at the drinking well at the foot of Baird's Brae. Thirsts were quenched before the sanctuary of Raglan Street. They were all in high spirits after their adventure.

Robert had a question for his big brother. "John, how did we go there? It wisnae a very nice place."

"Ah only wanted you tae see what it was like. You've not tae ever go there on your own. Ah need tae look after ye. Ah took ye there so you know where the bad places are. Do ye understand?"

"Aye, John. Ah didnae like that place but the fire was good. The deid dug was terrible. Whit a mess they boys made bursting it intae bits like that! Ah'm no going there again. They boys said they were gonny kill us. Were you no' scared, John?"

"Naw! Ah wisnae scared. They were only shouting their necks aff to chase us away. Ah wanted tae get you safe away frae there."

Recalling the warning from his mother, Robert asked another question, hoping for reassurance. "John? Was Joak Dan there?"

"Robert, Joak Dan's real but you never see him. You have tae stay away from places like that if ah'm no with ye. If you went there yourself, you'd meet boys like that and they would hurt ye! They'd be the same as Joak Dan, right? So you widnae have time to run away. You'd get caught and done up, and probably need tae go tae the hospital; mibby you'd even die! So you have tae watch and not get lost or go away too far on your own, right?"

"Okay, John. Ah'll stay wae you. Can we get up tae the house now? Ah'm cauld."

"C'mon then, ah'll race ye up the stair. Ah'll give you a start. Ready! Steady! Go!"

With the spell of serious talk broken, Robert trotted up the first thirteen steps, turned, and shouted cheerfully that John had no chance to win.

"You'll no catch me noo, John!" he screeched with the excitement of a six-year-old about to defeat his champion. He giggled and disappeared up the next flight of stairs.

John set off in pursuit, letting his brother stay ahead till the last flight before the top. Then he grabbed him by the pants, holding him back. This oft repeated game always ended in a dead heat. Robert took these races in good fun, but in his mind was an emergent desire; he aspired at some time in the future to win. He loved John. If his brother said it was right or wrong to do something, then Robert complied. He trusted John. He would go anywhere with him.

Paddy the Irishman

There was this big Irishman drover called Paddy. Every Saturday he drove his horse and cart on a vegetable delivery route that took him down Raglan Street. At Peggy Clark's grocery shop, John had offered to hold the reins. This became a regular habit. He showed no fear, even though his head barely reached the nose of the beast. He whispered to the horse and stroked its white face. Paddy knew the horse would not move away, even without this boy's help. He was impressed, though, by the affinity the boy had established with his huge animal. This led to John being invited to sit up beside the big fellow on the journey through the town. He would be gone for hours. This was one of those journeys that John knew his wee brother would love.

Accordingly, he had Robert beside him on Saturday when Paddy rolled into the street on his massive platform. He greeted John as usual, "Johnnie, me boyo! Top o' the mornin' to you. Who's your wee pal?"

"Hiya, Paddy! This is ma wee brother, Robert. Is it OK if he comes wae us the day?"

"Well now! Let me see him."

Paddy looked down at the tiny fair-haired boy and smiled. He had no trouble agreeing. Soon the two were seated up beside him on bales of straw, their legs dangling behind the horse's rear end. Robert was secure between Paddy and John. He leant back against sacks of potatoes. The straw bale scratched his bare legs, but he was content. This was a new adventure. He felt really important to be in this position, way up above the street beside Paddy.

Everything about Paddy was big. He had large hands, muscular arms, and a broad smiling face. His thick leather apron and shoulder protector were soft and scuffed like suede, with years of wear. His horse was a massive chestnut-brown Clydesdale that had long blond feathers from its knees to the ground. Brass ornaments adorned its girth straps and neck collar. It stood still like a statue until Paddy signalled it to 'Giddap!' Robert marvelled at the sheer strength as its huge rump strained in the shafts, its hooves scratching the cobbled road making sparks, until the whole rig lurched forward. Being up behind a horse this size was new to him. He had been on Kid McGlinn's wee cart, but his pony was tiny compared to this giant.

He was intrigued when he watched its tail rise up, but disgusted to see several round balls of bright yellow-green straw fall from its bum. Worse than that, it was accompanied by steam and a pungent smell.

"Awe, Paddy! That's stinkin'!"

John and Paddy laughed at the youngster's reaction.

"Sure now, it's only natural, Robert," said Paddy. "If yiz want to work with horses then yiz have to get used to that. Ye put straw in one end and straw comes out the other."

"Aye, but it smells a lot worse at the back, Paddy."

Paddy and John laughed at the kid's unintended joke. After an hour had gone. Paddy decided it was time for a bite to eat. He opened a paper bag and took out a thick cheese sandwich. He held it in his mouth ready to be eaten, and shoved the empty poke under his seat.

"Are yiz hungry at all?" he mumbled through the bread.

The boys were hungry but John, as always, said that he wasn't.

"Oim sure yiz would loik a little bite, now, would yiz not?" he countered.

The boys gave in, being unable to resist the offer of something to eat. Paddy broke his sandwich and gave each a piece. An hour after that, Robert was hungry again. He turned his smiling face up to his Irish benefactor.

"Paddy, have ye got any more pieces? Ah'm hungry again."

"Sure now, oi've not got a ting left, son. If oi had known you was comin' aboard oi would have made more. Oi'm sorry, boys," said the drover with genuine sadness.

They were silent as the cart rolled on. Paddy turned to the lads and said, "Does yiz loik potatoes, boys?"

"Oh aye. Ma mammy gives us totties at home. We love them," said John.

Paddy reached behind and lifted a sizeable new potato from one of the sacks. He let go of the reins, took the spud in both hands, twisted it quickly, cracked it into two pieces and handed them to the hungry boys. Robert looked at his half and then looked at John.

"It's no' cooked!" complained the boy.

John looked at him in horror. He was embarrassed at Robert's implied criticism of the Irishman's kindness. He needed to retrieve their amity, hoping Paddy had not been offended.

"We've ate raw carrots before. I think raw totties will be the same. Thanks, Paddy."

Then he smiled in an effort to disguise his distaste, and took a bite from the potato. Seeing this, Robert was reassured and copied him. To their surprise, both boys found that the cold potatoes were just like apples, but not so sweet. They were chewy and full of tangy moisture.

Paddy had not in the least been upset at Robert's remark. Watching these two urchins filling their bellies with his country's stable crop gave him a frisson of pride and delight. It was a pleasure to him having them aboard and helping with the horse. He was quite capable of doing all the work himself, but he was glad of their company. John did what he was told and was respectful. Not just to him…but also to his horse.

The big Irishman knew a bit of Irish history. Seeing the kids eating his potatoes reminded Paddy of the Irish potato famine, when the crops failed and people starved. *What a fine ting it is to have the power, with only a single potato, to satisfy the hunger of two scamps.* Within this thought, however, there was a tinge of sadness felt by the kind Irishman. He spoke to the boys as they ate.

"Oi've a little gem of a poem oi learned from me mother about the potato. Would yiz loik to hear it?"

Both boys, with starchy mouths, nodded in agreement.

Paddy went on:

"Where do you come from?"
"Donegal."
"How are your potatoes?"
"Fine and small."
"How do you eat them?"
"Skin and all!"
"Does that not hurt you?"
"Not at all!"

"Paddy, tell us that again. That's a great wee poem," said John.

The Irishman repeated it till they had both learned the words. They tried it and giggled at the sound of it. The boys sensed his joy and his easy attitude to them. The thought entered Robert's head, *if ah had a daddy, that's the way ah wid like him tae look at me.* That and other thoughts were in his mind as he stared up at the drover, watching as Paddy gently caressed the reins over the horse's rump. A proud grin softened up his usually stern big face. It widened when he heard Robert's verdict on the feast.

"These totties are smashin', Paddy, thanks a lot!"

Robert loved sharing escapades like this with John. He felt safe and had fun. It was not always the case. Sometimes life bit you!

Chivalry costs!

Before classes began in the primary school, the kids played games outside. When a teacher was spotted heading for the building, the kids raced to reach the school swing doors and get a *thank you* for holding one open. This was Robert's lucky day. He pulled on the high brass handle but could only pull the one heavy door ajar by a couple of inches. He instinctively put his left hand round the edge of the door and, with a huge effort, managed to get it opened enough for the teacher to slide through. She grabbed the handle as she went in, pulled the door shut and crushed the fingers of his left hand between the two doors.

"AAAAGGGGHHHHH! Ma fingers! Ma fingers! OOOHHHHH! Ma fingers!"

Oblivious to what she had done, she disappeared into the school. Another teacher arrived seconds later. Robert was so severely injured he could not be consoled. His sobs went on and on, even inside the headmaster's room. His left middle finger had taken all the force and its tip was swelled up to twice its normal size. The nail had been pulled but had not come off. It was a bloody mess. When Jeanie arrived, Robert had been bandaged up and sat quietly in the headmaster's room. She was not a happy woman.

"I want to know who did this to my son!" she demanded

"I assure you, Mrs Chessar, that it was clearly an accident."

"It had better have been an accident, Mr Kerr! No-one in their right mind would do this deliberately to anybody, never mind a child. Look at his finger. Who was it?"

"It's not possible to tell you, Mrs Chessar, because nobody knows. The person who did it seemingly doesn't know either. Robert was outside the door. The teacher who came in and closed the door must not have heard his cries of pain."

"Well, Mr Kerr! I find that very hard to believe. I don't care if it *was* an accident, but you mark my words, if I find the coward who did this to my boy and walked away, there will be more cries of pain, I assure you of that. And they *will* know who did it."

Mr Kerr was struck dumb by the force of this small woman's venom. Jeanie turned away and took her son home. A few days later, when he had quite recovered, he was back in school playing with John Carly, one of his pals,

"How's your sore finger, Robert?"

"It's OK, but under this bandage it's aw swollen up, look."

"See if that happened tae me, ma da would batter that teacher!"

"Ma m*ammy* said she would dae that. Ah've no *got* a daddy."

"How no'?"

"Ma mammy's been too busy looking after us aw. Mibbe she'll get one now that ah'm at school?"

"Wid you like a da?"

"Aye! A think ah'll ask ma mammy tae get one. Most ae ma pals have got one. He could teach me tae swim and buy me a bike. We'd need a bigger hoose, though. Mammy says oor's is full up and we'd need a lot o' money."

Buried treasure

After school, Robert ran home, rushed upstairs to his house, and asked his mother what she could give him for digging. He needed to go to look for buried treasure in the grounds of St Theresa's Church. She was sceptical but had no wish to discourage her son from such innocent work. *Hopefully it would keep him out of trouble for a while.* To humour him, she asked where he had gotten the idea for his intended excavation.

"Joe and Bertie said there's treasure buried in the grounds at St Theresa's Church. Ah'm going up there wae them tae find it, but ah need something tae dig with."

She handed over an old serving spoon and a fork, telling him to be back for his tea by five o'clock. She warned him that the Church had a clock so he would not be able to say he *didnae know the time*.

As he dashed out the door to his latest adventure, she joked, "Don't bring back too much gold. It's very heavy and I don't want you getting too tired for your tea."

"Awright, Mammy, ah'll just bring as much as ah can carry! Ah'll be able tae buy maself a bike and a fur coat for you as well."

It was a good distance up to the church. The three boys were keen to get digging. They trotted along at a steady pace, arriving out of breath at the gates leading into St Theresa's Park. They gazed at the expanse of grass skirted by a long driveway that ended outside a red brick building with a clock spire.

Robert said, "This is an awful big space. Where will we start?"

Joe said, "Where dae youse think the treasure'll be buried?"

"In among thae trees, ah suppose," said Bertie "C'mon an we'll jist pick wan tree an' start tae dig round it."

Soon they were hard at work with their assorted tools, hacking and scraping at the unyielding ground. After a while, they had a small hole and a little pile of earth.

Robert sighed, "This is hard work, intit?"

"Aye, and it's cauld here as well under the trees," said Joe with a shiver.

They changed their plan of attack. It would be better if they moved into the sunshine. They moved out from the trees to the other side of the driveway. The grassy ground there looked easier to dig up. They started to dig again, this time at the bottom of the fine green lawn that sloped down from the church. Enjoying the heat from the sun and finding the ground much more amenable to their small digging tools, they were soon down about six inches in a hole about a foot in diameter.

"Ah think there's something hard down in here," said Joe.

"Mibby it's a box wae the treasure!" Bertie said

More concerted digging revealed that it was only a stone. They continued to dig it out in the hope of finding the casket of gems. The eager diggers gave their full attention to the task. They were not aware of the tall male figure, dressed all in black, that had silently approached. As he watched what they were doing, he moved round slowly till the lowering evening sun cast his shadow over their worksite. Bertie looked up.

"Hello, mister."

Robert stopped digging and looked up. His first impression was that the black silhouette did not look friendly. *Is this Joak Dan? Am ah gonny die?* His mammy had been right. He should have been more careful. Now they were for it! The figure was too close, so they couldn't run away.

Just as Robert was about to yell for help, the shadow spoke. "Now, boys, why are you making a big hole in my grass?"

"We're digging for buried treasure, mister," they chorused, still not sure why this quiet presence had crept up on them.

Robert whined an excuse. "We didnae know this grass belonged tae anybody. Is this your grass?"

"No, it's not. It belongs to the church. But I suppose in a manner of speaking it is my grass because, you see, I am the priest who works in the church."

This information and his tone reassured Robert that this wasn't Joak Dan. He knew a priest wouldn't do anything bad tae them. Using his best smile, he offered a deal, "Well, see if we find any gold? We'll give some tae you for your church. Would that be OK?"

"I'm sure that would be fine," the priest agreed. "Are you boys intending to dig all over the lawn until you find your treasure?"

"Naw," said Robert. "We can only dig tae five o'clock. Then ah have tae go hame for ma tea."

"I'm very relieved to hear that. I wouldn't like you to be wearing yourselves out by digging up my whole garden. Since it is nearly five o'clock, why don't you stop now and run home?

"Oh! Mister, we're sorry we've made a mess. We thought if we found some gold that would make it awright. We'll fill up this hole and it'll look no bad," said Robert.

The boys got busy scooping back the earth and patting it down with their hands and spoons. The priest watched till they looked up again for approval.

"That looks fine. I will get the gardener to put some grass seed on it. When will you be back again to look for this hoard of gold and jewels?"

"We'll come back tomorrow, mister," said Bertie. His two kneeling companions nodded in agreement.

"You've done a grand job. Now off you go. Straight home now! Goodbye, boys, I'll see you tomorrow." But tomorrow was another day, treasure long forgotten.

That was scary for a while, thought Robert.

It had turned out all right in the end, but he had missed the presence of his big brother. *Wae John, I widnae have been scared in the least.*

Ghosts

He was soon to learn that his brother had another side to his character. Not a nasty side; more a misguided and mischievous one. On the frequent nights when Jeanie went out to the dancing, John and Jean were babysitters. They each sat on armchairs either side of the fireplace. Jean and John were normally good to Robert. John would die for his brother if he were in danger.

Tonight was different. They decided to torment him. Robert was in his pyjamas, being cuddled on his sister's knee.

He was only six, but they set out to terrify him with stories of ghosts. John pretended to be scared. He leaned forward with one hand over his mouth, pointed past Jean's chair, and shouted, "Look, Robert! There's a ghost behind you!"

Robert yelled in fear and ran to John's chair. His arms and legs formed a ball in his brother's lap.

Jean then screamed, "Look! Look! There's a ghost behind your chair!"

Robert was in her lap a second later, squirming with fear, seeking solace from his sister. Their laughter made him worse. The mischief continued till the boy was trembling with fright and sobbing out of control. They realised that they had gone too far. It was time to stop. It was time to begin their usual winding-down procedure – a cup of milk and a biscuit – but he refused that. This time, they were getting scared. Robert would simply not stop crying. They were unaware that the boy knew exactly what he was doing. He had figured out from several of these teasing sessions that there was no such thing as a ghost you could not see. This was the last time they were going to torment him. It was his chance to get his own back. When they both insisted they were only playing a joke, he jumped up and confronted the two bullies.

Feigning anger, he shouted with as much venom as a six-year-old could muster, "Ah'm gonny tell ma mammy on youse two!"

In one short sentence the tables turned on his tormentors. They realised they had to calm him down. Their mother was due home soon and Jeanie would be furious if she found out what they had been doing to her baby. There would be severe retribution. Their task now was to bring him back to normal, but it was too late. They heard the sound of the key in the lock in the front door. Jeanie was back! The kitchen door opened and the boy ran to her.

"Robert, why are you crying?"

"They two said there was ghosts tae frighten me, Mammy."

"We were only playing. He's just a big wean."

"I'll give you *'big wean'*, Jean. He's only six, and you're fourteen. I can see who the *big wean* is here. As for you, John, you are supposed to be looking after your wee brother, no' frightening the wee soul tae death. Look at him, the wean's terrified."

Robert's siblings were really getting the message from his mother. They stood looking very sheepish and mumbling, "Sorry! We'll no' do that again. Mammy."

"And another thing," shouted Jeanie, "He's supposed to be in his bed asleep by this time. How is he meant tae sleep when his head is full ae bloody ghosts? Come here, son, I'll get you a cup of milk and a biscuit. You two! Get through tae your bed!"

"Is he no' going tae bed wae us?" protested Jean.

"No! He'll sleep with Hetty and me tonight. Now, get out of my sight before I do something I'll regret."

While Jeanie was at the sink with her back to him, Robert caught the looks from his brother and sister and thumbed his nose at them. They thumbed back. Peace was restored.

In fact, Robert was not actually afraid of ghosts he could see. What frightened him during the torture sessions with Jean and John was the fear of the unknown. The one ghost this six-year-old had seen recently was his own property. It had come to him. He told no-one. He had identified with it. It was his personal guardian angel. He was not tormented much by his family. There were many times when the opposite was the case. There were many days of happiness and learning.

Nollie picnic

Hetty and Jean took Robert up to the canal bank for a picnic. Hetty bought a big tuppenny bag of broken biscuits from the cake shop in St. George's Road and a pint of milk from the dairy in Braco Street. With three cups from the house, they could look forward to a fine picnic up at the canal bank. The day was warm and sunny. Other folk were enjoying the quiet beauty of the place. They crossed the sturdy, arched wooden bridge to reach the grass. They found a good spot and settled down with their blanket and parcels of food to watch the activity round about. A barge boat was being hauled along the water by a rope tied to a Clydesdale horse on the far canal bank.

"Look at the size o' that horse, Hetty! It's as big as Paddy the Irishman's. It's pulling the boat."

"They're barges, Robert. They don't have engines, so they need the horses to move them."

"Ah'd love tae go on a barge. Can ah run across and see the horse?"

"Yes. Watch it disnae bite you," said Jean. "Look, there's another one coming the other way."

He trotted back over the bridge in time to meet the young boy leading the big horse. "Whit's your name?"

"Camlo. What's yours?"

"Robert." He replied. "Is that your daddy in the boat?"

"Yes. He is Cato."

Robert looked back to where the man stood on his barge and shouted, "Hello, mister!" When the man ignored him, he turned back to his new friend. "Whit's it like havin' a daddy?"

"What do you mean?"

"Well, ah've no' got a daddy."

"Everybody has a father. You cannot be here if you never had a father. Ask your mammy where he is. Maybe he went away."

"Naw. Ah've never had one. She wid've told me. Ah asked her and she looked as if she was gonny greet, so ah didnae ask her again. That's a smashing big horse. Is it yours?"

"No. It belongs to the family. We don't have personal things. It's all for the family."

"Can ah clap it?"

"Yes, at the front of his leg. Watch he doesn't stand on your foot."

Robert sidled along, half bent, beside the horse's front leg, stroking its long white hairs. He marvelled at the sheer power of the big beast and winced at the noise of its steel shoes scraping on the granite setts. They sometimes sparked if its hoof slipped.

"Your boat must be awfae heavy, but the horse disnae look very tired."

Camlo smiled at his companion. "The barge has fifteen tons of coal in it. The water takes most of the weight of the coal, but my big strong Angus still has to work hard to earn his hay. He is doing a fine day's work pulling it along here."

As the barge neared the bridge, Cato rang a brass hand-bell to warn the lockkeeper. He was already out with his mate and had the bridge up just in time. It opened from the centre into two halves.

Camlo shouted to Robert, "Stand well back! I need to stop Angus, and lift the rope over the bridge."

Robert watched with admiration as Camlo used a long pole to lift the slackening towrope up and over the upright half of the bridge. Cato steered through the narrow gap into the basin on the far side, moving steadily towards the oncoming boat. Camlo lifted his rope over the other horse while his father lifted it over the other boat. They passed by and headed on along the bank and away from Robert.

Camlo turned and shouted, "Cheerio, Robert! I hope you get a daddy soon."

"Cheerio, Camlo. Cheerio, mister." But again he was ignored.

The youngster ran back to his sisters. They were lying on the blanket with their eyes closed, oblivious to his visit with the gypsy boy and his horse. He lay down between them to relish the warm sunshine and dozed off. He awoke with his nose being tickled.

"Wake up, sleepyhead," said Jean. "It's time to go home."

He sat up and stretched, wriggling his shoulders to speed the process of shaking off his stiffness, saying through a wide yawn, "Hetty, ah'm thirsty."

"Okay then. Let's pack up and you can drink from the well at the foot of the brae."

Robert took the bulky pewter cup in both hands and gulped down a long cold drink.

"Oh!" he gasped. "That's nice!"

It was on days like this that he appreciated being in a world he felt was designed to give him pleasure. If that was not the case, then how else could he be so happy and contented? But he was young and optimistic. He was living his life from day to day, not making any plans or dreaming of any lofty ambitions, only the usual ones. He would love to have had a daddy like Camlo; a big strong man who trusted him enough to allow him to take complete control of such a big horse. *That would be great*, thought the youngster. *And a bike!* He would love to have his very own bicycle and be able to ride away on it all day long and go where he pleased. Maybe one day. He was learning *patience*. That was the nearest thing to an antidote for yearning.

FIVE
1949

Robert's sense of wellbeing took many forms. It was a particular pleasure of his to be in bed on schooldays, lying snug and warm between his brother and sister.

Clip-clop

Jeanie worked in a central kitchen in Thurso Street in Partick, where meals were made and then distributed by lorries to feed children at the school canteens. She had to be at work by seven o'clock in the morning so that meals went out by lunchtime. Robert was used to being woken up around six o'clock in the morning by his mother clumping down the stairs on her way to work. Her wooden clogs made her sound like a small horse as she clip-clopped down the stone stairs. He listened to her noisily crossing Raglan Street, through Braco Street, and into St George's Road. She had to be at the tram stop on time. If she missed the tram, she would be late for her work and lose some pay. She didn't earn much, so any deduction in her money was sore.

Her son listened until the sound of her clogs died away. Only when he heard the noise of the tram arriving was he happy that his mammy had made it. Then he could snuggle in between Jean and John, pleased that he still had another two hours in his bed before getting up for school. His life was sweet. He also loved running about with his pack of unruly schoolboy pals, playing games and getting up to mischief. They were a motley bunch of strong-willed youngsters, determined to squeeze the most out of every free hour of their days, especially in summer time. These were long days full of fun and adventure that stretched their abilities and imaginations. They took advantage of challenges offered free-of-charge by their environment. There were dangers, but they had few inhibitions about taking calculated risks in pursuit of their mainly innocent pleasures.

Cowboys and Indians

School was out and the shout went up, "Who's goin' up the Nollie?"

The Forth and Clyde Canal was known in the local dialect as *'the c'nawl'*. Thus was derived the expression, *'The Nollie'*. Near the canal bank, at the top of Baird's Brae, was a walled-in scrapyard, heavily overgrown with weeds, nettles, thistles, and jaggy brambles. Obsolete broken-down vehicles of an earlier era were dumped there and left to rot. To the youngsters, these old horse-drawn vans resembled the stagecoaches they saw in the cowboy films in the Saturday fleapit cinemas. Access was over a padlocked wooden gate, with barbed wire rolled over the top. This was no barrier to these nimble urchins. Once safely inside, they played out their cowboy games without fear of punishment for any damage they inflicted on the wasted wagons. If anyone got hurt, then the Oakbank Hospital was only yards away.

Ian Jordan shouted, "Ah've been stung wae nettles. Look! Ma leg's aw blisters."

"Get some dock leaves fae over there," ordered John Carly. "Rub them on his leg. That takes the sting oot."

"Hey, that's brilliant!" said Ian. "How did you know that?"

"It's a trick ma brother showed me when ah got stung once. It's good, intit?"

"Aye, it's no' half. A wish ah had long troosers, but. They nettles sting like fuck, so they dae."

After this truce in the wars, the fighting resumed with the usual sound effects. The kids imagining driving fantastic black horses between the broken shafts, manes flying in the wind, nostrils flaring, the cowboys shooting at the pursuing Indians, most would obediently died in a hail of bullets from extended index fingers to the sound of gunfire from pursed lips.

"Peeaaawww! Peeaaawww!" sang the boys, imitating the bullets ricocheting around the battlefield.

"Ah shot you! Yer deid!"

"Naw ye didnae! Ye missed!

"Ah shot you twice! Lie doon you, you're deid!

"You're deid! Ah got you wae an arra! You lie doon!"

"If you don't lie doon, yer no playin' any mair!"

"That's no fair, cos ah got you wi ma bow'n arra!"

"Ah goat you first. Noo lie doon an die cos yer deid, ya wee dick!"

"Ah told you, ye missed!"

"A'right then! Bang! *Noo* yer deid! Lie doon!"

So they played on with their simple rules till hunger reminded them that it was time for getting back home.

"Ah'm gaun hame," declared one.

The hostilities fizzled out and the boys, like a gang of mischievous meercats, streamed towards the rickety double gates. Undeterred by barbed wire, they cascaded over with experienced ease. Drinks were quaffed from the pewter cup at the well at the foot of the brae, then Robert and the gang flowed like sheep back down to Raglan Street. He enjoyed the sensation of speed, with the warm, early evening air blowing through his blond hair. He felt like a little stallion he had seen in one of the Western films, galloping with head held high to escape the baddies.

He darted at top speed into his close, and expertly scaled the thirteen steps to the first landing. The window opening was boarded up to half its height with wooden planks. Jumping onto this barrier, he clung to the top edge, pulled himself up, and eased his head and shoulders over the top. Looking down from fifteen feet up and seeing no-one there, he spent a moment to scan the backcourt, his home territory. The midden was tidy. The 'Midgy Men' had been the night before. The bins were empty and placed back inside the brick shelter. This pleased him. He was naturally tidy, and appreciated the thoroughness of the 'scaffies'. The adjoining washhouse was always tidy as it was still used by the neighbours. They kept it clean, and more importantly, kept it locked!

The sloping roof of the washhouse had once been clad with slates, but they had gone before Robert's time. Now they were covered with big stove-enamelled metal sheets, with advertising logos like 'Virol' and 'Camp Coffee'. He jumped down from his window perch and bounded up the next five flights of stairs to arrive, quite out of breath, at his front door on the top landing. He chapped on his door and waited, panting, until his mammy opened it.

"Hello, son. Have you run up all those stairs? Come on in and get your tea. Wash your hands first. Where have you been?"

"Ah've been up at the Nollie, Mammy," he answered matter-of-factly. "We were playing on the stagecoaches behind The Astoria Picture hoose. Ian Jordan got stung on the leg wae nettles. John Carly rubbed it wae 'dock leaves' and it got better!"

"You need to be careful up there, son. It's very dangerous! You never know who might be waiting to hurt you in those places."

"We're OK, Mammy, there's always a crowd of us. And if anybody tries anything, we'll aw run away."

In an effort to stress the danger of out-of-the-way places, without frightening him too much, Jeanie warned him again about the bad man. "Well, you just wait! If Joak Dan comes to find you, then you'll know all about it!"

She got his attention. He stopped washing his hands. Slowly, and with a look of apprehension on his face, he turned round asking, "You told me aboot him once before, Mammy. Whit will Joak Dan do tae me?"

She whispered, "He's the man in black, remember? He hides in the shadows or in the bushes. He waits to catch wee boys and takes them away."

"Away?" Robert whispered back. "Where tae?"

"Nobody knows, son, but they never come back! So you make sure he doesn't catch you. I've told your big brother about him as well. All right?"

With eyes wide as saucers, his answer was barely audible, "Okay, Mammy. John told me aboot him up at Jack's Mountain."

"That's good, son. Now, are you ready for your tea?" she said, breaking the spell.

"Aye, Mammy. What is it?" the relieved boy asked.

"Mince and totties and peas."

"Oh! Ah love mince'n totties. Have you put onions in it?"

"No, son. I've cooked yours separately, so you'll not get any onions."

Robert took his seat at the table. "Mammy?"

"Yes, son, what is it?"

"Is there really a Joak Dan?"

"If you're bad and go to places you're not supposed to, then you might get caught by him! But if you do as you're told then you'll be all right. Do you understand, son?"

"Aye, Mammy," he said with respect, but with a trace of uncertainty. He was not entirely sure where the right and wrong places were. He continued his meal in silence, still considering the implications of being taken away by this mysterious bad person. He tried to think of anyone who had recently disappeared.

When his sisters arrived, he asked if they knew about Joak Dan. They were unaware of the previous talk he had had with his mother. Hetty and Jean told him that they knew of no-one who had been taken away by the fiendish demon. A quick look from Jeanie, however, prompted them to tell their wee brother that there was always a first time, and he should be very careful because Joak Dan was indeed a real person.

"Will he come intae the hoose?" asked the wide-eyed Robert.

He was assured that Joak Dan would not bother him in the house or any place where he was allowed to go. But the same warning was reinforced regarding places that were out-of-bounds. Satisfied with their advice, Robert finished his meal. He cleared the table of dirty dishes over to the black sink, to be washed, dried, and put away in the cabinet, ready for breakfast time. He went to bed that night with his brain still considering the existence and possible danger of this bad man, Joak Dan. He would still run with the crowd back up to the canal for more fun and games, but he wouldn't mention his mother's warning because he thought they might laugh at him for being a scaredy-cat. *Never mind them, ah'll still keep a lookout for Joak Dan.* Next morning, he had forgotten all about him.

Tying doors

Robert was with John and a mob of older boys who were organising a well-tested game: tying two door-handles together with a rope. The doors on the tenement landings faced each other and opened inwards. To promote a result, the doors were kicked and the kids scampered to a safe distance to enjoy the ensuing noisy mayhem from the distraught folk trapped in their own homes, unable to open their doors. There were two problems to this game. Firstly, if the two doors on the ground floor were tied, the tenants could climb out of their front or back room windows and catch the little bandits unawares. Secondly (and this presented the gang with a further thrill), someone had to go in to untie the rope. These boys were childishly wicked, but still had a collective conscience. Who would be the lucky one to go in and risk being caught and dealt with?

A democratic method of selection was used. An older boy could volunteer to show how brave he was. Either that, or he told a youngster to do it or he would get bashed and put out of the gang. Big Danny, a proven coward, turned to Robert.

"Robert Chessar, you're gaun in tae untie the ropes!"

"Naw he's no'!" said John.

"He's never done it before, Chessar! It's his turn!"

"Danny! He's no daen it! You dae it! That is, if you're brave enough?"

Robert stood aside while this exchange took place. He was well aware that Danny was no match for his big brother, and that Danny would have to comply or look stupid in front of the whole gang. Mingling with the boy's quiet thought process was the growing chorus of the rest of the clan.

Getting louder with each incantation, they chanted, "Danny canny dae it! Danny canny dae it!"

Big Danny relented. He had no choice but to take up the challenge or be ridiculed and known forever as the big hard man with the soft centre. He spat his next words at John, "Awright! You win, Chessar! Ah'm no scared!"

He ran into the close and up the stairs to the first landing to untie one of the doors. Unfortunately for him, one of the trapped tenants was a strong man. He had pulled so hard that his neighbour's door-handle had been torn off. The man stepped out of his house just as big Danny arrived and caught him by the front of his jersey.

"Right, ye wee basturd! This is for being a fucking wee pest! You can give some ae this tae that wee gang ae fuckers in the street!"

With those few words, he began his assault on Danny's bum with his boot, kicking him all the way down the stairs, through the close, and into the street. He was greeted with cheers from the rest of the miscreants who were standing a very safe flight-distance from the close.

Robert turned to his brother. "John, thanks for saving me."

"It's awright, Robert. Danny's big enough. He can take it. You're too wee the noo for that kind ae thing. Never be forced tae dae anything you don't want to, and don't get intae fights you know you canny win – like Danny jist did. OK?"

Robert absorbed this good advice and made a mental note to avoid fighting or volunteering for anything whenever possible.

White horse

"Pick a number between ten and fifty, Robert," said Carly.

"Fifty-two."

"Naw, ya dope! Fifty-two's too high."

"Awright then, thirty-two."

"OK. Thirty-two it is. Who's gonnae be the white horse?"

Several non-takers made their wishes known. A round of 'eeny-meeny-miney-moh' finally isolated the fall guy, and Marshall Cower was sent to his fate up close number 32.

"Run up tae the top landing. When ye hear us shouting, *White Horse,* you run down as fast as ye can, OK?"

Marshall thought, *That's easy!* Obediently, he ran up the stairs…right to the top. That's when the gang standing in the close kicked the two doors and shouted *White Horse!* They watched from across the street to see the fun when Cower arrived at the foot of the stairs just as Mister Henderson and Missis Baker came out to see who had bashed their doors.

Hearing the noisy footsteps coming down the stairs, they turned and grabbed Marshall, the *White Horse!*

"Were you banging our doors, ye wee wretch?" said the man.

"No, mister. I was picked to be the *White Horse!* Those boys across the street must have done it."

The man thought for a moment before giving the boy a resounding slap behind his head, heard by the now jeering crowd outside.

"Ah canny skelp them, so you're getting it."

"And here's one from me as well!" said Missis Baker. And she landed a fine skelp to his rear end, to another chorus of approval from the villains.

Robert made himself a promise. He would never agree to be a *White Horse!* He would always be a spectator. It was safer. And it was more fun.

Revenge

Jeanie's neighbours, across the top landing, were the Buckleys –husband, wife, the granny who ran the sweet shop at the close, and three schoolchildren. The Buckleys kept themselves to themselves and made no attempt to interact with Robert's family. They had good money coming in. Their kids were well turned out, wearing only new clothes and shoes. The youngest, William, was ages with Robert, but William was discouraged form bringing Robert into his house. *He's not the type of boy we want our William to befriend.*

In spite of this, the boys sometimes played together. Robert, however, did not mistake the occasional clear signals from his pal's sneering looks that William Buckley felt superior. It was inevitable then that they often fell out. When you fell out in Raglan Street, you either ran away or you stood to fight. Being well aware of the Chessars' reputation as fighters, William always ran away. Robert always gave chase. Just as he was catching up, William always managed to run into his granny's shop.

Robert had to stop at the door, frustrated and angry. Barclay was safe for the moment under his granny's protection. Robert waited. His adversary was bound to emerge.

William's granny shouted, "Robert Chessar! Go away, you ruffian. Leave William alone. You Chessars are all the same. Just hooligans! I'll tell your mother."

"Ah'll get you when you come out, Buckley! Your gonnae get it!"

William, out of sight of the granny, stuck out his tongue and screwed up his face in a twisted smile of triumph, silently ridiculing Robert's predicament. This served to aggravate Robert even more. He was boiling with rage. This had happened many times. He showed a clenched fist to William, signifying he would leave revenge till later. He knew the only way to deny Buckley his sanctuary was to catch him before he got to his granny's shop. *Next time,* he thought, *that's what ah'll dae.* In the way of things, he was soon distracted by some other adventure. This latest spat was forgotten. But it was not the last.

The next time came soon. The bold William once again outran Robert and gained the inner sanctum of the shop. He turned round as usual to stick out his tongue and make the assortment of twisted facial gestures at Robert, in the certain knowledge that his attacker had to stop and be powerless at the doorway. He was, though, about to learn that such assumptions of safety are not always reliable. He turned and was surprised to see that Robert had developed an alternative battle strategy. Robert was face-to-face with him.

He gasped, "You're not allowed in here, Robert Chessar! Granny! He's going to hit me!"

Robert said nothing. He was savouring the imminent moment of triumph. The two boys stood eye-to-eye like two cats, each weighing up the other. One was feral, the other cringing. Robert was deciding which part of William Buckley was going to get punched first. William was thinking the same thing and was wide eyed with fright. The Granny was struggling to gain her composure. It was hard for her to accept that this fiery little devil had the temerity to chase her grandson right into her shop. This angry breaker of holy sanctuary was about to paste her beloved grandson.

She started to shout her usual command, "Robert Chessar—"

Just as the first blow landed squarely on William's open mouth.

"You get out of—"

Just as the second fist landed sideways on Williams left eye.

"Here. You dirty little—"

Just as Robert kicked William on the shin.

"Scoundrel!"

Finished, the granny struggled, with both hands in the air, to negotiate her little fat body round the small shop to get to her grandson's aid. With a look of victorious accomplishment, Robert slowly turned and took his leave of the shop. The low sobs and whimpers of William Buckley accompanied his leisurely exit. For this, and all past wrongdoings by the cheeky but now snivelling little smart arse and his bossy dictatorial granny, Robert's terrible appetite for vengeance had, finally, been assuaged. His family honour was well and truly satisfied. He had no further trouble from William Buckley. After that day, Robert bought his sweets from Mary Began's shop further up the street.

Brave Mountaineers

Mooching about around the streets could become boring for the local children if there was nothing happening. So, when any workmen came to carry out repairs, there was always a gang of kids gathered to watch and ask questions. Their curiosity always seemed to cheer the men up as they worked their magic with the likes of road drilling, melting tar in a boiler, or mixing and spreading concrete to fix the pavements. Robert's mother considered the smell of sulphur to be beneficial to health.

> "Get a good sniff of that 'tarry boiler',
> Robert. It'll clear your lungs."

The fact that the smell was actually quite pleasant meant the boy had no problem with doing as he was bid. He became fascinated watching while a new railing was being replaced at the church in St George's Road. The tradesman put a small cast iron pot over a gas torch to melt little bars of lead solder. He cleared the small recess for the railing and held it in place while pouring some of the glistening hot silver metal round it. In seconds it had set. By watching and asking questions, these different skills were learned and enjoyed, giving the boys ideas for jobs when they grew up. One exception was roof repairers. There was no chance to get up close to the men who fixed the tenements' roofs. Such a high and dangerous place was utterly out of bounds. It was so dangerous that there were no incidents of children being found on or having fallen off any roofs in the Raglan street area for as long as anyone could remember.

Robert and his brother were leaving the house after tea to go out to play. Tradesmen had left a ladder and some materials tied securely to the bannister on the landing, ready to continue their work the next day.

John said, "Hello. That's a handy ladder."

They went to the street and rounded up some troops. John put an idea to the gang. *We can use the ladder tae get intae the attic and look through the skylight to see what it's like up on the roof.* They assembled and climbed into the loft. The open access door gave some meagre light from the gas lamp on the stair. They found the roof skylight window and pushed it open, revealing the darkening evening sky. John raised himself through the tight aperture. Sitting with his legs dangling in, he looked over his shoulder to survey the street.

He exclaimed, "Christ! It's high up here!"

"Whit's it like, John? Are ye scared?" asked Big Danny.

"Naw, no really, but ah'll want tae get on tae the top o' the roof. Ah don't want tae slide aff these slates. Come on up. Bring ma wee brother up first so ah kin get him on the top beside me. Ah want him tae see this view."

Robert was pushed and pulled upwards till he sat beside his brother astride the ridge of the roof. Big Danny and two others struggled up and joined them, the five boys on the topmost part of their house like riders on a giant horse. Brave mountaineers! The sky got darker. They watched as the lamplighter, oblivious to his audience, moved down the street lighting the gas lamps.

One of them started to shout at people down below, "Hi! Doon there! We're the kings o' the castle, an' youse are dirty wee rascals!"

They *were* the kings of their castle. The folk in the street were unable to see them in the gloaming, and wondered where on earth the shouts were coming from. Sitting on the cold apex of the roof, like riding a seaside donkey, was to Robert the most exciting thing he had so far done in his life. He saw Raglan Street on one side and Lion Street on the other. He could see the trams ablaze with lights, making their way from Garscube Road up to Keppochhill Road.

He shouted with joy, "Hooray! John, we're nearly up tae God."

"Aye, Roburt, but hing on tight or you'll be nearly down tae the devil!"

Danny's foot loosened a slate. It slithered noisily down the roof, over the edge, and fell clattering into the middle of Raglan Street.

"Danny! For fuck sake! Ye could kill somebody."

"Ah don't care! Don't you shout at me, Chessar, or the next thing aff here'll be you!"

"You'll need an army, ye daft basturd. Shut your mouth!"

It was dark now. Stars were out. They had become too boisterous for John's liking. He decided that they had had enough excitement. He manoeuvred to a sitting position on the skylight to help each one down into the attic. Safely on the stairhead, he closed the hatch. His altercation with Danny was over. Big words and fighting talk don't always end in battles. John knew that, anyway, because Big Danny was a coward. They ran down the stairs and emerged from the close. On the other side of the street stood a group of adults talking and pointing up at the roof. The boys walked over to them.

John asked them, "What are ye lookin' at?"

Several adults all spoke at the same time in a jumble of words.

"There's some weans up on that roof, and its fifty feet up!"

"They're going to get themselves killed if they don't come down this minute!"

"I think someone should get the fire brigade or the police!"

"It's an absolute disgrace that these kids can get up on tae a roof like that!"

"Who knows what damage they can dae? A slate's already fell aff!"

"Someone's going to get hurt or killed!"

"Do you know who they are?"

Robert's big brother took the question in his stride, answering quietly, "Naw. Would ye like me tae go up and find out?"

"Absolutely not! Let them get killed if they want. Don't be going and risking your life for those stupid idiots."

John exclaimed in mock shock, "Aye, you're quite right, mister! Only a bunch o' dopes would go up on thae roofs?"

He sauntered away, leaving the concerned onlookers none the wiser. Although they were fairly proud of their adventure and felt brave and animated for having done it, the words of the people in the street had made an impression.

John offered his opinion to the group. "It *is* daft tae climb roofs. It is even *dafter* tae dae it *twice!*"

Fitness training

There were advantages to living in the top flat of a tenement. It was quieter at night, being further away from the noises in the streets. It was also marginally safer being further away from the people in the street and from the fact that only one set of neighbours ever passed your door. But there were disadvantages.

"Robert, take the ashes down to the midden, son, there's a good boy."

This chore completed, he ran back up to the house with the bucket, to be met with another polite request. "Robert, would you run up to Peggy Clark's and get me a stone of totties, there's a good boy?"

This was no mean achievement for a seven-year-old. He willingly did as he was bid, returning – complete with the

77

change – breathing hard but fit as a fiddle. Many times the mains water supply was cut off for some repair. This meant another chore. He and his brother were sent to the fire station in St George's Road to bring back two pails of water for cooking and washing. They were supplied with shiny galvanised pails at the fire station.

The youngsters struggled home with the buckets, losing most of the water on the way. To reach their top flat meant climbing fifty-nine steps. Robert did that many times a day: to go to school and back; to go to the shop for a message for his mother – a pint of milk; a loaf of bread; a newspaper from Wee Willie Knox at the top of the street; for some cigarettes from Mary Began's; and finally, to go out after tea to play. Before the age of eight, Robert had run up these fifty-nine stairs at least five thousand times, making approximately three hundred thousand steps. Each being eight inches high gives a height of two hundred thousand feet.

It follows that long before Sir Edmund Hillary had climbed Everest, Robert and his pals had all climbed nearly seven times the equivalent of Mount Everest! Robert was fit as a flea, and his climbing skills were called into play one day to save Hetty and Jean from a terrifying little monster.

Cat and mouse

It was on a quiet Saturday, when Jean was not fighting with Hetty but co-operating to clean the house. Robert was seated at the table enjoying the peace. The two housemaids were getting along quite well. The tranquillity was shattered by Jean's piercing scream as she jumped onto the armchair by the fireplace. Hetty let out another scream and, clutching her skirt to her knees, commandeered the other chair, yelling, "Robert! Get it! Hurry up! It's in the fireplace! Catch it! Catch it!"

He couldn't believe that he was watching his grown-up sisters jumping up and down on his mother's good chairs, calling for his help. He came round to see what horror in the hearth was causing this terror. When he saw it, he scoffed at them, "It's only a wee moose!"

While Jean and Hetty screeched at him to do something, he formed an idea. But seeing the state of his sisters, he thought it best just to do it rather than waste time trying to explain. They were in no mood for listening to reason, having lost their own. He simply said, "Okay!"

Then he ran to the door, ignoring their pleas not to leave them. The quicker he got on with it the better. He flew as fast as he could go, down the fifty-nine stairs, emerging in the backcourt to hunt for a cat. He knew that cats kill mice. Logically, if he caught one and took it up to the house, it would do that for which it was designed. He soon spotted a likely candidate. It was black and not too big, resting as cats do, enjoying the warm ground on which it was languishing. It looked easy to entice and hopefully be persuaded to co-operate. He went down on his hunkers with his left hand on his knee. His right hand was extended towards the pussycat, his thumb gently rubbing on the other fingertips.

Robert whispered endearingly, "Chih! Chih! Chih!"

The cat's ears twitched. Its head turned. Attracted by this curious gesture by the small boy, it mewed a greeting.

Robert increased the lure, knowing from experience that this wee beauty was about to be his. He spoke softly, "C'moan, pussy! Chih! Chih! Chih!"

Stretching its front paws while raising its haunches, the cat yawned, stood up, mewed again, and strolled up to him to rub its head on his hand. When it purred, he knew he had it. He stroked it and lifted it gently into his arms where it was happy to nestle. In less than two minutes he was back up the stairs and bounded into the kitchen, not bothering to shut the door. He was amazed to see the mouse still crouched in the fireplace. He crept over and presented the cat's nose to the mouse.

"Right, pussy, here's a moose for ye!"

The mouse was six inches away from its whiskers. The cat went rigid. It seemed to be stuck where it was. It was even resisting the boy's attempts to push it forward. He was annoyed that it did not immediately spring into action and kill the mouse. What was wrong with a cat that saw a mouse right there for the taking and was frozen to the spot? Hetty and Jean continued to plead with him to do something.

He complained, "This cat's nae use! It's feart frae a wee moose!"

Suddenly the cat shot forward from Robert's grasp, grabbed the mouse, and sat there holding it clenched in its mouth. Robert was ecstatic as he shouted out, "Look at that! It's caught the moose! Ah think it's deid! Well done, cat!"

A split second later, the smart cat scurried out of the open doors and shot down the stairs with its prize. The sisters came down off the chairs. They were back to normal at last. Robert was satisfied by his ingenious solution to their problem. His prize was a penny. That would soon buy him a buttermilk dainty caramel from Mary Began's sweetie shop. Before he went to buy it, Robert noticed that the two sisters were, for once, sitting facing each other excitedly talking and giggling about the cat and the mouse. He thought this was nice to see because it was so unusual.

Crockery

The rivalry between Hetty and Jean was legend. They were like oil and water. Jean was a tomboy and a tearaway, and Hetty agreed with her mother that young Jean was mixing with the wrong people. Wee Jeanie was at the end of her tether trying to control her. It was so hard to keep the two sisters from squabbling. Young Jean resented Hetty being the second-in-command in the house. It had been the same when their dad was alive. Robert and John had no memories of their father, but Jean could recall having some good times with him. Her resentment for Hetty had begun at that earlier age when she realised her big sister was her daddy's favourite. Hetty was the one who had known her father for twelve years before he was killed in the war. Jean was only eight when he died.

Hetty was the one who had corresponded with him when he was in the army. And Hetty started work at fourteen in Boots the Chemists, so she was earning for the family long before Jean even left school. Those unhappy feelings had grown over the years. Now aged fourteen, Jean's anger was part of her character. She bickered with Hetty almost every time they spoke; usually because Hetty would order her to do things rather than ask her. When they sensed the tension starting to mount, the two boys made themselves scarce. The best place to go was into the other room. The arguments would start quietly, but it was never long before there was a full-scale shouting match.

Jean was disadvantaged when it came a battle of wits. Hetty had an armoury of arguments to counter any of Jean's. The inevitable result was Jean becoming more frustrated at losing another *verbal* battle. Her last resort was violence.

One day, Robert was the only witness in the house, watching these two having a war. Hetty decided she had had enough of her sister. At the height of her destruction of Jean's character, she stormed from the house, slamming the outside door. Jean clenched her fists above her head. She had been ready to explode with anger and attack her sister. Hetty's high-handed exit made her scream with rage. Robert heard a very long, drawn-out, high-pitched squeal of defeat and fury. He put his hands to his ears and shut his eyes to block this terrifying sight and sound. Then things got worse.

Jean opened the kitchen cabinet to get at her mother's dinner dishes. She picked out a plate and flung it the length of the room. It smashed to smithereens on the door. Robert opened his eyes to see the shards of the white plate falling to the floor around him. Jean felt some relief from her destructive action. Another plate was dispatched to the same fate. Her wee brother burst into tears for the loss of his mother's plates.

Sobbing with fear at the shower of broken crockery, the terrified boy pleaded, "Jean! Stop it! You're breckin' aw ma mammy's dishes!"

She paid no heed. Plate after plate and all available missiles were launched in a steady stream at the door. This continued until there was not one left. Not one plate, cup, saucer, milk jug, sugar bowl (complete with sugar), sauce bottle, or jam jar survived the short journey to the kitchen door. The pile of broken glass and sticky mess surrounded the trembling boy. Jean, drained of passion and out of ammunition, stood still. Robert wept.

He pulled the kitchen door open, noisily scraping away the heap of stuff at its base. He went down the stairs to the close, wondering where to go. He walked to the foot of the street and up to his Auntie Maggie's house. He knocked at the door and waited. His Auntie Maggie opened the door and saw immediately that something was very wrong.

"Oh, it's wee Robert. Come in, son, what's the matter? Has somebody hit you?"

"Jean's broke aw ma mammy's dishes!" he managed through his new sobs.

Maggie put her arm round him and ushered him to a seat at the table, while her daughter was sent right away to Jeanie's house to find out what had happened. Maggie took a wet facecloth to her nephew, dried him with a towel, and got him a biscuit and a glass of milk. When he had calmed down, she got a better account of Jean's dirty work. Maggie skilfully got him to talk about other things, taking his mind from his horrific experience. Meanwhile, Jeanie had been home, got the gist from Maggie's daughter, chased young Jean out of the house and set about tidying up the mess.

Later on, she came to collect Robert, telling Maggie that it was all sorted. The situation had been dealt with.

"What about young Jean? Is she alright, Jeanie?"

"No. I don't know where she's gone. Ah kicked her out the house."

Thereupon the tough wee Jeanie burst into tears. "What am I going to do, Maggie?"

"Well, the first thing is to stop greeting. Here, take my hankie. Next thing is tae get a cup of tea. Then you can get Robert home and talk to Hetty about what to do with your daughter. Think about why she's done what she's done, and try to sort it out for the benefit of your four weans, Jean included."

"I don't want her back in the house, Maggie, but where would she go if ah don't let her back?"

"She'll have tae come back. She's got nowhere tae go. This is only a few dishes. We'll give you some tae see ye through. Ah'm sure Katie and Lizzie will have some old ones they'll no miss. You'll get by, and in a day or two this will all be forgotten. Now drink up your tea and ah'll see you up the road."

Robert was glad when he got home and saw the mess was cleared up. Maggie took young Jean over to her Granny Campbell's house, and it was agreed she could stay there for a few days till this all blew over. To everyone's surprise, the girl was so helpful at her granny's house that she stayed a lot longer. She was not suffering the repression of her big sister any more, and relished being virtually *the only child*.

About two weeks later, a tea chest was delivered to 27 Raglan Street. Two men carried in the box and put it down in the middle of the kitchen. Hetty signed for it and they left. Jeanie, assisted by her three remaining kids, opened the box to reveal its gleaming white porcelain contents: six dinner plates; six soup plates; six pudding plates; six cups; six saucers; six side plates; a large milk jug; a small milk jug; a sugar bowl; two soup tureens with lids; two baking bowls; two pudding bowls; a cruet set; a big teapot; and a white porcelain rolling pin with brown wooden handles.

The boys were overjoyed to see this entirely brand-new set of dishes. The wooden tea chest was *almost* new. It was lined with fine clean tissue paper, and at the bottom it still had some tealeaves. Robert loved the unexpected aroma that remained in the box. Hetty had got the new dishes from a mail order catalogue. She was able to pay for them over a period of twenty weeks out of her wages. Jeanie smiled at the feeling of sheer luxury she got from having these new dishes. The kitchen cabinet was only big enough for the plates and cups. The rest went into the sideboard. Balls of tissue paper lying all over the floor were soon stuffed back into the tea chest, and Jeanie used her new teapot to brew a pot of tea. The four of them sat round the fire drinking from new teacups. Hetty and Jeanie relaxed in the chairs, the boys reclined on the carpet.

It was then, during their reflective silence, that John noticed the borrowed dishes piled on top of the sideboard.

"Have we tae take they old dishes back tae Auntie Maggie?"

"I don't think so," said Jeanie.

"Well," said the boy, "we can give them tae Jean and she can smash them!"

Hetty and his mother began to laugh. They stopped when a quiet little voice piped up. "That isnae funny, John!" said Robert.

"Quite right, son," said his mother, stroking his hair. "She'll no' break another dish in this house!"

When he was in bed that night, Robert was feeling aggrieved that his mother had not sent his sister to jail. What she had done was very bad. He had been badly frightened by her smashing those dishes. It cost Hetty and his mother a lot of money. She should be punished for it. If Jean was sent to the jail, that would save money. That money could be used to buy him a bike, and for a while there would be peace in the house. He had a child's sense of justice and fair play. He was angry, but kept this to himself. *If any o' my pals hurt me like Jean had, ah would make sure they paid for it.* He didn't have long to wait for his chance.

Retribution

While he was at school, Robert was obliged to be polite and attentive. Jeanie told him that was how to get into the good books of his teachers. So far, he'd had no trouble with any of them. Miss Crabtree, however, was the exception. For some reason known only to her, she had a dislike of him. One of the boys in his class, who came from the bottom of Raglan Street, was known to be this teacher's pet. His name was Marshall Cower, a smart boy who always wore new clothes. Robert was tidy in his second-hand clothes. Because he had the edge with Miss Crabtree, Marshall looked down on boys like Robert. The two boys were not actual enemies but were far from being friends.

It nevertheless came as a shock to Robert when Cower stood up in class one day and said, "Please, Miss Crabtree, Robert Chessar called me a bad word."

"Oh? And pray tell me what that was, Marshall?"

"It's a very bad word, miss, I can't say it out loud."

"Well, you just come out here and whisper it to me."

He whispered the word in her ear but just loud enough for the whole class to hear as his eyes locked with Robert's. "Bastard, miss."

The class gasped in mock surprise. They all knew the word but were wise enough to show innocent horror. They had little idea of its meaning.

Robert was non-plussed by the sheer audacity of his accuser and shouted, "Ah never called him a basturd, miss!"

"Robert Chessar! That is a very bad word, and I will not tolerate such language in this school!"

She had accepted, without question, the word of the other boy.

Robert blurted out again in a defiant attempt to defend his honour. He was telling the truth, but the teacher would have none of it against the word of the clean and decent Marshall Cower. "But, miss, ah didnae call him a basturd."

"You come out to the front of this class, Robert Chessar. How dare you use that word in here? You are a very naughty boy, and I am going to give you the tawse to teach you that we do not have that kind of language used in our class."

She reached into her desk to bring out the leather strap. "Hold out your hand!"

He complied and, without flinching, received a whack on his right palm.

"And the other hand, please!"

He took the same on his left hand without a murmur. His eyes released a tear, showing that he had been hurt. The teacher decided that he had been given enough. She did not know that the tears were not from the pain. These were tears of frustration at not being believed by her. and the liar, Marshall Cower, had fooled her into believing his lie. Robert got unjustly strapped and ridiculed in front of the class. He was helpless to prove his innocence.

The afternoon continued with the two boys exchanging glances across the room. Robert was letting Cower know by his clenched fist below the desk that he would soon have his revenge when school was out. Cower's earlier look of triumph was now one of foreboding. The little liar may have cleverly outclassed Robert, but he was going to learn a thing or two about one-to-one combat when he was outside the sanctuary of the school. He now knew he was in a bad situation, being aware of Robert's reputation as a fighter. He was remembering a boy who'd tried to steal Chessar's playpiece and ended up lying crying on the ground with a bloody nose. He was not looking forward to the end of this school day. Perhaps he had been wrong to lie to the teacher. The only thing for it was to make a run for it at the final bell.

The moment came. The school bell rang. The teacher dismissed the class and Cower was off in a flash. Robert was ten yards behind him when they left the school playground. He had caught up five yards by the top of Balnain Street. Running across North Woodside Road, he was at Marshall's heels. By the time Cower reached his close, Robert had caught him by the jacket and swung him round against the wall. With a look of terror, he stared into Robert's snarling face. His usually tidy hair had fallen down over his eyes. Robert smiled at the sight, grabbed his tie at the neck, and raised his fist.

Marshall began to cry. Robert looked down. Water was pouring from Marshall's trousers. With a mixture of disgust and surprise he scoffed, "You've peed yourself."

Cower was trembling with fright, waiting for the beating he so richly deserved. He pleaded with his furious attacker, "Please don't hit me!"

Baring his teeth and spitting his anger in the face of the now petrified boy, Robert yelled, "You told the teacher a lie aboot me. You're the basturd!"

"Chessar! You've made me wet my trousers."

Robert released him and stood back. He felt a tinge of regret for shaming his prey this way. He had the better of him. He had his victory. The state Cower was in was adequate revenge for two of the belt. He gave a stark warning.

"You're no worth hitting, Cower. Next time you tell lies about me, ah'll kill you!"

There was no next time. Cower gave Chessar a wide berth. Robert's sister Hetty, however, was not so kind with another attacker.

Poor May Hughes

Just like the wise old priest at St Theresa's Church, lots of people in Robert's life stirred warm feelings in the boy. May Hughes was not one of them. She was a widow who had moved into the house below Jeanie's when his Auntie Katie moved back to stay with his Granny Campbell. May was always complaining about something or another. Robert and John were the usual subjects of her diatribes to their mother. In her estimation, *they were making her life a misery.* Jeanie Chessar was a distant cousin; Hughes was May's maiden name. She had two children who were called Buchanan, but when she lost her husband, she returned to her maiden name. She was the daughter of a brother-in-law of Robert's grandfather. Because of that loose relationship, the Chessar children were given to calling her Auntie May. Her own father, Jock Hughes, was an old man who lived with her. He was a kind old fellow.

Jock Hughes was quite famous. One day, years before, he caught a drayman in Raglan Street savagely whipping his horse. Jock yelled at him to stop beating his animal. The man turned on him. Jock laid him out. The police were called. The brewery bosses were horrified at the horse's wounds. So impressed were they by Jock's pugnacious defence of the beast, they sacked the drayman and employed Jock in his place. He looked after the big Clydesdale for many years before retiring. This was a typical example of the old school of men born in the nineteenth century... courageous, kind, and dignified. Robert was always pleased to see the old chap and to say hello to him, and enjoyed getting a friendly pat on the head.

May Hughes, on the other hand, was a woman who whinged about everything. She would chap up through the ceiling if Jeanie's two boys made any noise above her when Jeanie was out for a wee break at the dancing. Seconds after Jeanie came back, there would be a loud persistent banging at the door. Jeanie guessed what was coming.

"I suppose that'll be May Hughes. What have you two been up to?"

"Nothing, Mammy," came the standard reply from two innocent faces.

May started on their mother with a high-pitched tirade about the noise and mayhem the two boys made in Jeanie's absence. When she left, the house got back to normal. Her complaints were unfair because the boys were mostly quiet. There was sometimes a bit of horseplay, but surely not the racket that May insisted had been going on. During one of her visitations, she was in full flow with her noisy complaint.

"You know, Jeanie, these boys o' yours are completely out o' control. It's OK for you. You get out tae your dancing, but ah've tae stay in to look after ma faither."

"Yes, May. I'm sorry if they caused a wee bit noise. I'll talk to them."

"Talk tae them? You should be skelping their arses. That's what they need!"

"I'll decide what they need May. Leave it to me."

"You need a man in this hoose. He would sort out thae two rascals!"

May was nearly past the point of just *talking*. Jeanie tried to take the heat out of this tirade. She wanted no violence, and certainly not in front of her family.

"Hetty. Put the kettle on, love. We'll have a cup of tea. Calm down, May, you seem a wee bit frustrated. Maybe *you* need a man?"

Hetty put the kettle on the cooker with the gas full up to get it ready quickly. May Hughes did not let up in her haranguing of her mother. She delivered her next speech in a high-flown tone.

"You've a cheek saying I need a man, Jean Chessar. Ah haven't got four unruly weans doing just what they like in this house when their mother is out gallivanting all over the place cavorting with who knows who!"

Hetty had heard enough! Every time May Hughes came to the house, it was to complain. Every time she complained, it got worse, became louder and more abusive to her mother and the rest of the family. There was little her mother could do to resolve the problem, as it was not possible to comply with May Hughes's demands for complete silence from their house.

Jeanie tried again to placate the irate widow. "May! I think you've said enough!"

Hetty lifted the teapot from the cooker. It was half full of cold tea and tealeaves from the previous brew. She turned to rinse this cold mess into the sink. She hesitated for a moment, just at the point when May had reached a crescendo of her whining, grumbling protestations.

"Well! I am only just starting. It's time somebody told you the truth about your household!"

That's it! thought Hetty. *She's gone too far this time! It's about time somebody taught May Hughes a lesson she'll not forget in a hurry.* In an instant, Hetty turned and tipped out the teapot. Not into the sink, but all over May Hughes! The big noisy shouting head of the grumbling woman from downstairs was drenched in cold tealeaves. The silence lasted for a few seconds, then May shrieked loud, long, and high!

"Jeanie Chessar!" she screamed. "You've not heard the last of this! That daughter of yours should be in jail!"

Jeanie struggled to get up to help her, but sat down again. She was helpless with laughter at what had just taken place. Robert, John, and Hetty left the kitchen very quickly and ran into the bedroom, leaving their hysterical mother to sort it out. The noise from the kitchen was a mixture of their mother's shrill laughter and her attempts to placate the wretched woman.

May got up and rushed to escape. As she opened the door to leave, she gave a pathetic threat, "I'll see your weans in a home, so help me!"

Jeanie was not overawed by such idle talk. "May! You've only got what you deserved. You've made my life a bloody misery for years. If anybody needs the jail, it's you! Don't come back here again, or next time the tea willnae be cold!" Jeanie slammed the door shut.

The very next week, while Jeanie was out at the dancing, John was instructed to wash Robert in the bath. The two-handled zinc bath was put down in front of the fireplace. The kettle and a couple of pots were on the gas cooker, warming up. Robert was sitting on the armchair wrapped in a towel, waiting for his tub to be prepared. The coals in the grate were burning nicely so Robert would be warm when he got into the water. John mixed the hot and cold water and tested the temperature with his elbow. Sunlight soap flakes were added, bubbles made, and Robert hunkered down into the welcome suds. He enjoyed the infrequent luxury of having a bath at home.

John let him splash away happily in front of the fire. He stood up so John could wash him all over. John was rubbing him with soap when Robert lost his footing. He slipped and fell towards the fire. Instantly, with the reflexes of a cat, John grabbed him and pulled him back. They both fell away from the fire. The bath came with them. Both were soaked. John grabbed a towel and wrapped it round his brother, making sure he was not hurt.

They stood and watched the gallons of soapy water seeping through the holes in the linoleum, through the floorboards, down through to the ceiling of the house below. Auntie May's house! It was clean when it left the bath. On its route to her house, it not only took away the dirt from their floor, but it went through the sound-deadening ashes that filled the floor void between them and the house below. It was bound to emerge in May's house as a dirty, dark stream from the hole in her ceiling where her light was fitted.

John knew it would take a few minutes to make its downward journey. He urged Robert to get dried while he put the bath away. Then he dried the floor with the towel and hid it under the bed. He expected any second to find Auntie May banging on the door. She never appeared.

She had waited till she heard Jeanie on the stair, and mentioned something about dirty water. Jeanie was bewildered. When she got up to her house, she queried John, "Do you two know anything about May getting water through her ceiling?"

John looked bewildered. Robert mirrored his expression, looking angelic. John spoke.

"Water through the ceiling? How could that happen unless it came fae our house?"

Robert thought, *Ma big brother is really clever. Told the truth but gets away wae it.*

Jeanie thought, *It couldnae have come from us. I would have noticed.*

This was Jeanie at her best; protecting her family, knowing full well what had happened. She rarely missed anything her boys had done, but she was not going to admit anything to *that crabbit-face down the stair*. It was nearly seven years since Jeanie had lost her man in the war. May Hughes's man had died too; probably to get away from her nagging tongue.

Jeanie put on the kettle for a cup of tea. Sitting with it by the fire, she mused, *any man would have to be desperate to take up with that bitch. It'll take a special man to replace my John; somebody might come along and sweep me off my feet. After all, I'm only forty years old. You never know.*

Uncle Frank

Jeanie kept up her visits to the dancing and came home one night to reveal news that startled Hetty. She was unaware that her mother had been seeing the same man for a while.

"I've grown very fond of this man, Frank, and he has asked me to go on holiday with him for two weeks in Ireland."

Hetty was horrified. "You can't do that, Mum! It's scandalous!"

"Why can't ah do what ah want? It's my life and it's about time I got a wee bit of pleasure out of it."

"Mum, you will be away with him in a hotel. You'll be sleeping in the same bed. You can't go. It's disgraceful!"

"Hetty, I've not been in bed with a man since your father was killed. It wasn't disgraceful when I went tae bed with your daddy and had four weans as a result. You're nineteen now, and are old enough to know what goes on between a man and a woman."

"Mum! I'm shocked at you. When you had us, you were married."

"Well, ah'm not married now. If I want to have some fun out of life, it's actually none of your business."

"If you come back from Ireland pregnant, you will be the talk of the street. That *is* my business. People will be laughing at us. That's the *last* thing we need."

"Don't be daft! We will not have that problem. I know what I'm doing, so there's nothing you can say that will change my mind."

"Mum, I think you're making a big mistake. And another thing…who's going to look after Robert while you are away globetrotting with this Frank what's-his-name that we haven't even met?"

Jeanie dropped another bombshell. "Robert is going with us!"

"Oh! I suppose he will sleep in-between you and Frank?"

"No, Hetty, he will have his own room. That way, Frank and me will have complete privacy to do what we want. Now, just get used to it. I am doing what I am allowed to do. Please stop trying to prevent me. It won't work."

Hetty gave up and stormed out of the house. It was not like her to stand up to Jeanie as strongly as that. She was a decent, clean-living teenager, and truly shocked at her mother's intentions. She believed it would bring shame on her and the rest of the family.

Jeanie sighed and sat down. She had expected no less than a robust response from her eldest daughter. *But I've sacrificed half of my adult life rearing these four weans. I just want to feel human for a wee while. Surely they don't grudge me that?*

Robert was in bed sleeping soundly between young Jean and John. Jeanie was certain that he would like being on holiday with her and Frank. She would use their time on holiday to tell him about his father. He was still unaware that he had ever had one, so patience would be required. *That may not be so easy,* she thought. He would be difficult to placate if he took the news the wrong way. Still, it had to be done sometime and this seemed like a good opportunity. Frank would help. He was a solid fellow – a farmer from Ayrshire, steady and reliable.

Jeanie took her son to Hoey's the outfitters at St George's Cross to kit him out for his holiday. They were to stay in a posh hotel and she was not going to embarrass him by having him wear second-hand Raglan Street clothes. This would be costly, but she had a bit put away for a rainy day. He got a pair of navy-blue shorts, socks, pants, and two white short-sleeved shirts. In the shoe department, he got sandshoes and new sandals with silver buckles. The black school trench coat he had got from his Granny Campbell's recent 'bundle' was almost brand new. He would look smart in it. Her son was looking forward to meeting Frank. Jeanie treated herself as well. This trip might change their life.

The following Friday night saw Robert on the Broomielaw quay at the River Clyde. He held tight to his mother's hand and his small suitcase. They met Frank and waited in a queue ready to board the overnight steamer to Dublin.

Robert looked up at the ship. "Mammy?"

"What?"

"This boat's as big as Raglan Street!"

"Aye, so it is, son. It takes a lot of people, so it has to be big."

"Mammy? How dis it no sink intae the water?"

"It floats because it hasn't got any holes in it," said Frank.

"Frank? Are you ma daddy?"

"No, Robert, Frank is like your uncle."

"But, Mammy, ah've already goat an Uncle Frank."

"Yes, but now you've got two. Okay?"

"Okay. Hello Uncle Frank. Ah'm Roburt."

Frank was tickled pink with this wee fellow's directness as he shook the small proffered hand. "Very pleased to meet you, Bobby."

"Naw! It's Roburt! Don't call me Bobby, that's a name fur a dug!"

"Sorry! Robert it is then. We are going to get on just fine you and me. Aren't we?"

Robert, still holding his mother's hand, looked up at him, smiled, and said, "I'd like that."

During their overnight sail, Robert slept on a couch in the ship's lounge. The ship docked mid-morning at Dun Laoghaire (pronounced-Dunleary) harbour. A short taxi ride had them at the foot of the steps to their hotel. It was three storeys high, a terraced villa, cream-painted, and looking like a palace. Inside, the lady owner greeted them warmly and led them up to their rooms. Robert glanced down through the balustrade at a boy standing in the hall looking up at him. He returned the boy's short wave. *Someone to play with,* he thought. They entered a large room with a wide bay window overlooking the street. A double bed, bigger than any Robert had ever seen, took his immediate attention.

"Mammy? There's only one bed. Have ah tae sleep in it wae you?"

"Oh no, young man," said the lady, reaching for his hand. "You will have your own room next door. Come with me and I'll show you."

He was led away while Frank and Jeanie took possession of the cupboards and drawers of their suite. In the adjacent room, he stood and looked without a word. The owner took his case and put his clothes into one of the big drawers. She took off his coat and put it on a hanger inside the wardrobe. He still stood looking. This room was the size of his whole house in Raglan Street. It could not possibly be for him alone. Finally, with the lady touching his shoulder and inclining towards his surprised looking face, Robert spoke.

"Who aw sleeps in here, missis?"

"What do you mean, son?"

"That bed. Ten folk could sleep in there. Dis that boy down the stair sleep here as well as me?"

"No, son, it's your bed. This room is for you. It's yours for two weeks till you go home again with your mummy and daddy."

"He's no ma daddy, he's my Uncle Frank. Ah hivnae got a daddy, missis. But ah love this room. Thanks very much."

"Oh! I see."

With a knowing look she turned to leave. "I'll just close your door, Robert, and you can make yourself at home."

Robert went round the room exploring every cupboard and drawer. He liked being treated like a prince. His room, she said. His bed, she said. Your door, she said. All this was his for two weeks. That was fine by him. For two whole weeks he would revel in his newfound luxury. After that it would be, as his mother often said, *back tae auld claes* (clothes) *and porridge!*

It had been quite a journey. Although tired, Jeanie and Frank decided they had time to venture out for a short walk in the cold morning air to explore the harbour town. Robert was more than happy to play with the boy he met; the nine-year-old son of the owner. He had shown Robert the boxes of games inside the sideboard in the lounge, and they went wild, running up the stairs and sliding down the banister.

When Frank and Jeanie were ready to go, she called him. "Come on, son. Get your coat. It's time to go."

Robert said cheerio to his new pal. He held his mum and Frank's hands. The farmer had broad but gentle hands. It was raining. Not heavy rain; gentle drizzle that seemed worse than rain. It stuck to Robert's clothes, but he was well wrapped up in his navy-blue raincoat and school cap. He was comfortable between his two adults. He smiled up at Frank as he skipped up the slight hill to the main street. Although he was only seven, Robert had by now astutely realised that his new Uncle Frank could easily be wrapped round a kid's finger. In the town, at the express demand of the boy, Frank bought him a toy car with a wind-up, clockwork motor.

Frank took them to the seashore, but it was a disappointment. There was no sand. The spray from the waves was flying up over big rocks the size of cars. The toy car slipped down into a deep cleft. It could be seen but not reached, and the sea was throwing salty water all over it. Robert started to moan that he wanted it back. Frank lay down and stretched as far as he could, trying to reach it, but failed. The car was lost, he said.

Robert would not accept this, however, and made his feelings known to his submissive uncle.

"Aw, Uncle Frank, ah don't want tae leave ma motor here. I want it back. Can you no' get it back for me, please?"

Frank's coat was soaked but he accepted the challenge. He found a washed-up fish box bound with wire, and smashed it with his feet and hands. Robert was impressed. The sides of the box, still with bits of the wire to hold them together, extended to more than the depth to reach the car. Making a hook with the wire, Frank again lay down and, using this long wooden lance, managed after several attempts to lift the car back into the boy's hands.

During those two weeks, Robert luxuriated every night in his huge bed, feeling very pleased with himself. Before falling asleep, he relived the adventures he was having there in Ireland: the rocky shore; the strange continual rain and wind that never seemed to bother him or the two adults; the ride on the elephant in Phoenix Park in Dublin; the visit to the Guinness brewery, where he was allowed to knock blazes out of a piano while his mammy and Frank went into the beer section; all the fun in the hotel with his pal; not to mention the great food he was getting. In this two-week holiday, he was remembering especially the bits involving Uncle Frank. He thought, to start with, that Frank was going to be his father.

Then Jeanie took time to explain how he already had a father, who had been killed in the war the same year Robert was born. He reasoned that if he were going to have a new father (who would really be his first one) then Uncle Frank would be very acceptable. Robert had warm feelings for this man, who bought him stuff when he wanted it. He was certainly a strong and brave man, rescuing his toy car the way he had done, against the onslaught of the sea amongst dangerous boulders. He hadn't seemed to mind that he got soaked in the process. That impressed the youngster.

Robert felt closer to his 'uncle' Frank than he did to any of his *real* uncles. Frank often lifted him up, swung him round, tickled him, ruffled his hair – all these things that endear a man to a child. This made Robert feel wanted and even loved. He had never had that before. He imagined sometimes that if he had ever had a 'daddy', then this is what he would have done. How could he *not* like a man with such longed-for appeal? Frank had a quiet reassuring voice. His face was kind. He had lines on it that made him seem to be smiling even when he wasn't. When he did smile, his face lit up and Robert couldn't help smiling back at him. Frank's eyes were green the same as his own.

"Robert, you must be from Irish stock with those green eyes of yours."

"Yours are green tae, Uncle Frank."

"Right enough, Robert, but maybe there's also a wee bit of the German in you, with your blond hair and handsome face," said Frank, with a pull on the boy's ear.

Robert laughed innocently at that and the cheeky nip from his uncle. Jeanie, on the other hand, would not have Robert compared to a German. Her retort to Frank was short and sharp,

"There's no German in my son!"

Robert was unmoved by the references to Germans, and playfully grabbed Frank's hair. It was black and crinkled with small curls, soft to touch, and smelled of tobacco. That aroma reminded him of his mother. How happy he was during his walks in the street between these two, holding a hand each, and feeling protected on both sides. He was free to swing and jump and be a part of a unity that he had never felt before.

When they started to get ready to come back home, he asked his mother the thing she may not have wanted to hear.

"Mammy?"

"Yes, son."

"Will Uncle Frank be ma daddy when we get hame?"

"Would you like that, Robert?"

"Aye. He's great fun. Ah like him a lot, Mammy. Ah think John would like him as well."

"I like him, too, son. More than you know."

Their journey home ended with a taxi ride to Raglan Street. Frank patted Robert's head and Robert gave him a hug.

Frank hugged Jeanie and went back into the taxi. Before he shut the door, he said to them, "Robert. Thanks very much, son, for a lovely holiday. It was great fun."

"Thanks, Uncle Frank. I hope we see you soon?"

"We'll see, son. Jeanie, don't forget to talk to Hetty."

"No, ah won't, Frank. Thanks for everything. I'll phone you in a week or so."

Frank smiled and shut the door. The cab slowly exited Raglan Street, taking Frank away to the station for his train back to Ayrshire. Jeanie took her son up to the house. The place was all spic and span. Hetty had been busy as usual, making sure her mother would have nothing to do but relax after her long journey.

A few days later, Robert was through the room. He heard raised voices from the kitchen. This was surprising, because young Jean, normally the instigator of loud arguments, was not at home. It was Hetty and his mother who were shouting. He crept into the lobby and listened at the kitchen door and heard Jeanie say, "What do you mean, *I canny get married*?"

"I didn't say that! I said you couldn't move to Ayrshire!"

"Why not? Frank has a farm, and it's big enough to have us all there as a family. What's wrong with that? It'll make things a lot easier for us all."

"I'll tell you what's wrong with that, Mum. I'll not be going there, and I don't think Jean will be going either. If you want to split us up, after keeping us together through thick and thin these last seven years, then you're going the right way about it!"

"But, Hetty, you must come with us. You can get a good job down there. There's bound tae be plenty of opportunities for you. It'll be good for Jean, as well as the two boys."

"My opportunities are with Collins Publishing. I'm secretary to Mr Woods, the divisional manager. If I go to Ayrshire, I'll lose my whole career. I won't be able to travel back and forth to Glasgow every day from away down there in the middle of nowhere!"

"Well, Hetty. It seems that it's you who wants to split this family up, not me!"

"That's not true, and you know it! Two years ago, I had the chance to take up a great job in London with Collins. You said you needed my salary in order to feed us and to keep the family together. That's what I've given up for this family. You can't ask me to give up the rest of my career prospects just so you can marry some guy we don't even know, and move to a bloody farmyard at the back of beyond!"

"Alright, Hetty. That's the end of it. You have given your best for us; there's no denying that. I'll phone Frank and tell him we can't see each other any more."

In the lobby, Robert cried quietly to himself. The subject of that fierce debate was the man with whom he had shared such a brief part of his childhood, but who had made such an impact on his life for those two short weeks of freedom from poverty and stress. Robert had hugged Frank and said cheerful goodbyes. He was unaware then, that he would never again see this man. He had never missed his real daddy because he had never known him, but he missed the man who had shown him such genuine affection – his 'uncle' Frank.

SIX
1950

As far as anybody knew, Jeanie never saw Frank again, but she continued going to the dance halls. She was a good ballroom dancer and enjoyed the buzz of the crowds, the music, a wee sherry on occasion, plus other things known only to her. She seemed happy with what she had achieved since the war ended. Hetty, on the other hand, was fast becoming a career girl in Collins. She had a circle of intelligent male and female friends, and also went dancing. One lad in particular took her fancy, but she was playing hard to get. Her career came first – an affair was low down on her list.

Young Jean, now out of school, worked in a dry-cleaner's shop for a while but found it hard to keep up with the discipline of work. Currently she had a job in the grocery store. John, now in Woodside Senior Secondary School, was miles away from his wee brother in Grove Street Primary. Robert still remembered his 'Uncle Frank' and the wonderful times they shared in Ireland, but he had no problems now about wanting a father. The one who was dead and buried meant nothing to him. Frank had been something else, but Robert had accepted he was not going to see him again. It had been a hard lesson for the boy and still hurt, but he was becoming tougher at dealing with disappointments in his life.

Out of school times, John tried to be with him as much as possible. They got into many scrapes and adventures with the other rascals of the street. John seemed to have an affinity for horses; probably from his times with Paddy the Irishman. He had become friendly with a sharp-witted boy down the street who had a pony and cart. He kept it stabled in a lane up near Camperdown Police Station.

Kid McGlynn

John's Auntie Maggie lived, one up, in the last close on the other side of the street, next to the old Davy's rag store. Up the same close lived Missus McGlynn. Her boy, known as Kid McGlynn, was older than John by three or four years. He was a real character. He whizzed around the Cowcaddens with his pony and cart, doing small and large removals for folk, sometimes moving a whole house of furniture. These were often done in darkness, if the people had fallen behind with their rent.

Robert first encountered this remarkable youth when he and John stood outside Kid's close looking at the pony. It stood munching on oatmeal from inside a leather bag hanging from its neck. Kid McGlynn came out of the close and saw John. He yelled, "Hiya, John, is this your youngster?"

"Aye, this is Robert. Can he come wae us for a hurl on the cart?"

McGlynn smiled at the tousle-haired eight-year-old and, like Paddy the Irishman, readily agreed. The three got up and sat on some straw-filled bags. Their feet hung down behind the rump of the pony. Robert felt safe in the middle. Kid brushed the reins gently on the animal's back. This was the pony's alert signal. It shook its head as if to complain that the nosebag was still round its neck.

Kid mumbled a quiet swearword in annoyance. "John, get the bag aff its heid, will ye?"

John jumped off, retrieved the bag of oats, tossed it onto the back of the empty cart, and got back up beside Robert. Kid gave him a knowing wink. He lifted the reins slowly and then slapped them hard onto the nag's rump. It reacted instantly and shot away at speed. Caught off guard, Robert rolled back onto the cart, yelling with surprise and fright. John had hold of his jersey and hauled him back up.

Robert giggled with the fun of his tumble. "Youse did that on purpose!"

The older boys laughed out loud and totally denied having tricked him. Kid said, "You'll need tae hold on a bit tighter, Robert. We don't want ye tae roll aff the back o' the cart."

They all laughed at that. Robert was pleased they had played a funny trick on him. He was cute enough to know there was no malice in it. It meant they liked him. That was all that mattered. He was in their gang; one of the gang. The cart was small, about ten feet long. The pneumatic tyres, unlike Paddy's the Irishman's ironclad wheels, made a smooth quiet ride apart from the slapping sound they made on the cobbles. The boys spent the whole morning whizzing around on the cart. Kid McGlynn uplifted and delivered bits of furniture from houses and boxes from shops. He collected cash-in-hand for each service. Try as they might, John and

Robert could not get him to say how much money he was making. That was a closely guarded secret. He wasn't being stingy or mean, just careful.

At one point, the rig was running down Maryhill Road. Kid pulled over into the left just past the Blythswood Cinema. Handing the reins to John, he got off and lifted Robert down to go with him. They ran across the street and went into a sweet shop. Kid asked for ten Woodbine cigarettes from a shelf behind the shopkeeper, and she turned round to get them. Quick as a flash, Kid moved his hand across the counter, like a bus driver turning his steering wheel. It was so fast that Robert wondered why he had done it. Before he could ask, the shopkeeper turned back with the cigarettes.

She asked, "Anything else?"

Kid shook his head, paid for his fags, smiled to the woman, took Robert's hand and left. Back on the wagon, he took his hand from his pocket and handed each of the boys a Fry's cream-filled chocolate bar. Taking the reins, he coaxed the horse to move off.

John said, "Thanks for the sweeties, Kid. Where did ye get them?"

"Ah bought them in that shop," Said Kid with a smile.

Robert knew that this was not true. He peeled the paper from the chocolate bar, took a bite, and said nothing. He just looked at the back end of Kid's pony, knowing intuitively that you don't look a gift horse in the mouth. He put his hand to his nose when its tail lifted.

Nollie Nookie

Next evening after teatime, the Raglan Street rascals ran up Baird's Brae to the canal bank to play near the bridge. They wandered a short way along the path towards the derelict warehouses. This quiet, secluded part of the waterway was a favourite place for courting couples. It was dark, for one thing; and it was cheaper than two back seats in the nearby Astoria picture house down the brae.

The bunch of boys were not looking for any trouble, but when they saw a man and a woman kissing and hugging in the seclusion of a shady corner, they huddled for a quick discussion. *Why was the man continually pressing himself against the girl, and why were his trousers around his knees?* It was evident to them that something unusual was going on. One boy suggested they were, *doing it.*

To various assorted queries, he responded by explaining that '*it*' was what dogs did to each other in the street! One remedy was to drench them with pails of cold water. That option held little appeal for the boys, as they had no buckets, and they would need to get up close and personal with the target. That would be too close for comfort. A more attractive solution was agreed. They would throw stones at the couple – partly to encourage them to cease their randy behaviour, but mainly just to spoil their fun.

By the time they agreed their plan, the amorous couple had reached a stage of some accelerated mutual interest, with attendant joyful noises. One of the boys picked up a pebble and threw it in their direction. It missed them, but hit the corrugated metal on the warehouse. Needless to say, the targets were by this time so engrossed in their activity that this missile and its sound effect went unnoticed. The lads were encouraged by the noise the stone had made, so launched a salvo of larger pebbles at the unfortunate lovers. Some hit the target but most of them rattled off the metal shed.

The male member of the courting pair was thus obliged to divert a portion of his attention to the attacking forces, while still attending to his duties for his ladylove. He wailed in helpless frustration, "Fuck aff, ya wee basturds!"

To a hearty chorus of jeers and yells of derision, the boys continued their assault on the hapless couple, in certain knowledge that, in his present predicament, the foul-mouthed suitor was not about to pursue them. To the obvious displeasure of his beloved, he continued to fire insults at the now riotous band of brigands who were so pitilessly pelting them. His insults to the boys were returned with interest.

"Get aff yer bike, mister!" cried one.

"Get aff the crossbar, missis, before ye brek it!" yelled another, before doubling up with a maniacal scream of laughter at his own joke.

Having now concluded that to continue his adventure with the lady was an unattainable dream, the Don Juan disengaged and began to retrieve his trousers. At this clear sign of a change in the tactical logistics, the gang turned like a flight of starlings, yelled their defiance, and ran for their lives along to Baird's Brae and downhill to safety.

Their jaunt at the canal was laughed and chatted about for a while back in Raglan Street, but it was soon forgotten;

replaced by other mischief. The two unfortunates on the canal bank probably would remember it for a long time after, but Robert's mischievous pals would never know…or care. It wasn't long, though, before Robert and his mates had another exciting adventure at the nearby bridge.

Skinny-dipping

Robert wished he could swim, but for some reason he had a morbid fear of the water. In the swimming baths his feet couldn't touch the bottom at the shallow end without his nose going under the water. This, he did not like. His brother, John, tried to help him.

"Use the steps and ease yourself into the water."

Robert shivered from fear and the cold water. The lapping waves felt like little monsters snatching at his shoulders. His arms became tense. He held tight to the metal rail, fearing if he let go he would drown.

"Just hold on, Robert. Let yourself go flat and kick your legs."

The youngster was not to know it then, but John's words would, one day very soon, echo in his head. For the moment, negativity filled his mind with doubt and fear. *This is never going to work. I'm just a coward. John is probably thinking the same.* Fear was winning. He tried to fight it, but it was hopeless. His brother's pals shouted encouragement, but this only added to his confusion and shame. *Ah'd love to show them all that ah'm brave.* He persevered, but he did not like being in the water one bit.

A few weeks later, as he stood on the canal bank beside the wee wooden footbridge, he was wrestling with those same feelings. He was fascinated, seeing his pals chucking off their clothes and jumping naked into the water. He watched them playing. It was late August. The sun had been warm and the evening was balmy. His mind was once again controlling his safety instinct. *I'm a coward. I canny do this.* His nearly nine-year-old brain could not understand why he was scared to death of water. These fears were real, but he didn't know why he had them. *Why me? Why can I no' just jump in and swim? It's no fair that I'm so different. All ma pals'll laugh at me. They'll know I'm a coward.*

He remembered nearly drowning in the Woodside Baths. His brother's repeated advice had not helped him. *Just lift your feet and you'll float, Robert. Just keep trying and you'll soon get the hang of it.* That had been a fateful day. Robert was eager to please. Keen to overcome his terror and the inhibiting sense of self-preservation, he forced himself to let go of the rail. But he didn't float. His body turned upside down! The sharp and clear noises of the people in the pool seemed to be coming from a long distance away – muffled; a sort of low droning, like his head was in a beehive. His eyes were open. Spinning round and round, he could see tiles everywhere. He was not aware of holding his breath, but he was aware of not regaining the surface of the water where he could grab the friendly rail. With arms flailing and legs kicking, he thought, *Ah'm gonny die!* Just as the drowning boy's mouth opened to inhale his last breath, John grabbed his protruding arm and hauled his wee brother onto the poolside.

Lying, gasping and terrified on the cold tiles, Robert began to sob, "You told me it was easy tae swim! Ah nearly drowned and it's aw your fault, John Chessar! Ah'm gonny tell Mammy on you."

Hugging his brother, John spoke softly. "Robert, Robert, you're aw right now. You're ma wee brother. Ah widnae let you drown."

The youngster calmed down. Crouching there, entwined together, dripping wet and getting colder, the pair formed an unbreakable bond. Robert had lost all desire to swim…but that was then.

Now, he was standing alone on the canal bank, still mortally afraid of the water. In spite of his pals cajoling him to join them, he showed no intention of getting in. He was also intensely shy of revealing his naked body to anyone. In any case, the canal water looked filthy. Watching his pals enjoying their noisy fun, impulsive childish thoughts sneaked into his head. *Maybe it might not be so bad. The night's warm. They big stanes along the side of the canal would be easy to hold on tae. It's getting dark. Dark enough to hide ma bare bum.*

"Come on in, Roburt. The waters no' cauld once you're in."

The encouraging shouts of his friends and their happy noises only served to increase his feelings of isolation. He didn't want to be outside the group or be ridiculed as a 'scaredy-cat'. Fighting his fears, he began to strip off his clothes. He piled them neatly on the bank beside the bridge. With his hands tactically placed to preserve his nakedness, he sat down on the cold edge-stone. Turning over onto his belly, he felt the rough sandstone scraping his skin. He giggled when he heard a pal shouting, "Hey, Roburt! We can see your bum!"

Gradually, he lowered his skinny frame into the water. More shouts came.

"Chessar's comin' in!"

"Well done, Boaby!"

"Don't let go! The watter's deep and you'll droon!"

Most of them knew he couldn't swim a stroke. He was shivering and holding tightly to the side wall. How good it was to feel part of this bunch and to hear their approval. But this cold dirty water was not to his liking. A few minutes later he shouted, "Ah'm freezing! Ah'm getting oot!"

Pulling himself up, he swung his legs onto the bank. When he stood up, he felt slightly dizzy, tottered backwards and fell – bum first – into the canal, making a loud splash.

"Robert's fell in! Quick! Get a haud o' him!"

There was a flurry of splashes as the gang swam like piranhas towards their friend. Robert heard none of that, being busy trying to find which way was up. This was not like the swimming baths. He could see nothing. He held his breath. He felt fearful again. It was then that his brother's voice echoed from far away, *Just let yourself go flat and kick your legs, Robert.*

The frantic noisy commotion of the gang on top of the water was producing no results. They could not see their pal, who was now deep down in the dark water. They swam round and round. Some dived down to grab anything that felt like a boy, but nothing was found. After a few seconds that seemed like hours, the boys began to climb out. They sat on the edge. They were silent.

While all of this was going on, Robert was doing his best to do what his ethereal voice had instructed, *Just let yourself go flat and kick your legs, Robert*. He let his body stretch out, and went flat. Instinctively, he stretched out his arms. He kicked his legs and started to go forwards. He had no idea of his direction. For all he knew, he could have been swimming along the canal and not across it.

He was not thinking about that. He was concentrating on moving to somewhere, but where? Then he saw a dim light. He had surfaced next to the side wall of the canal. Grabbing the wall and big breaths of air, he looked round to see where was. His pals were nowhere to be seen. He had swum under the bridge and surfaced on the other side of the canal. Stretching upwards, he dragged his weary body onto the bank. Rolling to safety and gathering dirt as he went, he warily stood up to ensure he was steady. It was quite dark by now.

Cold and naked, he crouched and tiptoed across the bridge. He stopped silently behind his friends. He heard one saying, "Who's gonny tell his mammy he's deid?"

"Who's deid?" queried Robert.

"Roburt's drooned in there."

"Naw ah'm no! Ah'm here behind youse. Ah swum under the bridge and got oot the other side. Ah can swim!"

There was no describing the jumble of feelings that erupted from the boys as they realised their pal was not dead. He had not drowned. They had no need to give bad news to his mammy. None of them would be in trouble. Most importantly…Robert had swum!

Using his vest, he dried off and started to get dressed. The others, by this time, had had enough and were in various stages of doing the same. They were quick to forget their frightening drama.

"Ma maw's gonny kill me!" said one.

"How?" queried his pal.

"'Cos ah'm manky, and ma claes are soaked!" he moaned.

Robert was thinking this, too, but his chief concern was how to tell his big brother the good news that he could swim. If he admitted being in the canal, he would be in big trouble. He decided this would be a secret known only to him…and six or seven pals. He was sure that his secret would be safe with them. They all assembled at the drinking fountain at the foot of the brae. Robert rinsed his hair, face, and legs, took a drink of the clean water, smiled, shivered, and ran with his pals back home to Raglan Street.

The Green Vindec

Robert was obsessed with bicycles, but he had to be content with renting them from the bike-hire shop in Cedar Street. It cost a shilling for an hour. Hetty taught him to ride a bike during a holiday at Dunoon when he was six. It was a gents' bike; so big that he had to put one leg through the frame, under the crossbar, to reach the other pedal. These early lessons began his love of speed and the freedom of being on a cycle by himself. On a hired bike, it was not possible to go far in an hour's rental, so like the rest of his friends, he just played around Raglan Street, screeching the tyres with skid turns in racing games. They had to keep returning to the shop to find out how much time was left.

"How long have ah got?"

"Twenty minutes, Robert."

Him and the rest of his pals were well known to the owners of the shop. When not actually on bikes, they hung about waiting for one to become available, or just hung about chatting to the man if they had run out of money. Robert loved the smell of oil and rubber in the shop. The old bikes lay at crazy angles against each other. The walls were festooned with spare wheels, inner tubes, tyres, frames, and everything you would need to build a whole bike. Many were damaged. The owners tried to keep them in good order, but the users treated them with scant respect with their robust use of them. When he went to hire one, Robert would arrive out of breath, clutching his shilling.

"Any bikes ready?"

"No' the noo, son."

"How long?"

"Let me see… Half an hour, Robert."

"Oh naw! Half an hour!

"Aye, sorry, son. We've got a lot that need fixing, so you'll have tae wait."

"Will you put ma name down?"

"There's three waiting already, so you're number four, Bobby."

"It's Roburt."

"Aye, ah know that, Bobby."

"It's Roburt! Bobby's a name fur a dug!"

The man laughed at this serious reprimand. The youngster was quite happy to be in there, hopefully not waiting too long for a machine. He chatted happily with the men in charge, watching them doing repairs. This was a good education for when he would have one of his own.

"Whit dae you call that bit there?"

"The crank. That round bit is the Sturmey-Archer gearbox."

"How's the saddle held on?"

"Look under it. See the round bits and the nuts through them?"

"Oh aye. Ah see them. If ye loosen them, it can be turned up or down?"

"That's right, Robert. We'll have to give you a job when ye grow up, eh?"

"Naw. Ah'll have a good trade wae lots ae money. Ah've promised tae buy ma mammy a fur coat."

"Whit kind ae fur coat is it she wants?"

"She says she wants a mink coat, but if ah've no goat enough money fur that, she says she'd be happy wae a beaver lamb. Ah don't know the difference, but."

"Mink's awfy dear. Beaver lamb's nice. Maybe you should get one o' them first. If she likes that, then you'll have saved yourself a right few shillings, Robert."

"That's a good idea. Then ah can buy ma bike as well, eh?"

"Now you're talking, son. We'll sell you one at a good price."

"Naw, ah'm gonny buy a new yin. It's gonny be a Vindec, the same as your green wan, except mine'll be red."

"Dis that mean oor bikes arnae good enough for you, Robert Chessar?"

"Aw naw! Yours are good the now, but ah want a new yin when ah'm big."

"Ah'll take that as a compliment."

The boys abused the bikes, using them for speedway, hard braking and skidding, hence the brakes and the tyres quickly wore out. If a bike came back needing serious repair, you got the blame and your name was put in 'the bad book'. That meant a period of waiting to get back into 'the good books'. The length of the sanction depended on the severity of the damage. Known offenders got the worst bikes.

The boys were choosy. The best bicycle in Cedar Street was an emerald green 'Vindec'. This was a gem of a machine, and it rode well. It had good cable brakes, straight pedals, droop handlebars with plastic grips, and a Sturmey-Archer three-speed gear that actually worked. It was a dream! When Robert went into the shop, he always hoped to get this one. When he appeared in the street with this bike, he heard, "Awe! Ya lucky pig, Chessar! You've got the green Vindec!"

Robert's angry response was, "It's fuck-all tae do wae luck! Ah waited a long time tae get it!"

Water bombs

When money was short, youngsters invented games that didn't cost anything. There was also a safety in numbers within a group of mischief-makers. Robert's brother and some others were gathered on the top of a washhouse in a backcourt down the street. From this vantage point, they could see dimly into the ground floor house of an old couple. The top half of their window was fully open due to the hot summer weather. Mr MacKay came into the backcourt and shouted up at the noisy crowd.

"Hey! You lot! Get down from that roof, and stop looking intae our house. Come on now. Off the roof and away and play somewhere else."

"We're no' doin' any harm up here. We're only playing, mister. We canny see intae yer house, honest! It's too sunny. Anyway, we're allowed up here."

These were honest replies. The boys were making paper water bombs in preparation for a coming battle. They were in the process of filling them with clean water using lemonade bottles. It's never wise to threaten a potential enemy who has a superior force, has commandeered the high ground, and also has possession of a plentiful supply of weapons and ammunition. It was at that exact moment that Mr MacKay, not being a military man, made just such a tactical blunder.

"If youse don't come down now, I'm going to get the police to you!

He had drawn a line in the sand: *obey me now, or suffer the consequences*. A water bomb, intended to be used in a battle between the rivals on the roof, hit Mr MacKay full in the face. Mrs MacKay, who had just then emerged from the close, exploded with rage.

"You wee pigs! Get down from there and stop your nonsense. Look at what you've done to my man; he's soaked. John, go in and get dried. If youse don't stop all this, I *will* go for the police."

Now that was a poor idea. It was very easy if you had a phone, but most houses didn't even have electricity never mind a telephone. To get the police, you used the phone attached to a police box. That got you connected with the Northern or Camperdown police stations. Neither the old man nor his wife was showing any sign of leaving the scene to go to the police box in Lion Street. It was some distance away. The streetwise gang was confident there was no immediate danger from the *boys in blue*.

"Away ye go then. Where are ye gonnae find a polisman, missis?"

One youngster glanced at the open window of the old folk's house. The top half of the sash window was down. Encouraged by his gang's noisy bravado, he shouted to the angry woman, "We're gonny throw a bomb intae your hoose, missis!"

This outrageous rant so appealed to the rest of the boys on the roof, that they started to sing in unison:

"We're gonny throw a bomb intae your hoose!"
"We're gonny throw a bomb intae your hoose!"
"We're gonny throw a bomb!"
"We're gonny throw a bomb!"
"We're gonny throw a bomb intae your hoose!"

This had a startling effect on the old couple. They turned, mumbling some unintelligible expletives, and hirpled back through the close to what they thought was the safety of their house. The loud chanting continued unabated. Mr MacKay feared the threat from the marauders was real, so he clambered up onto his sink to try to close the top half of the window. He got a shock as soon as his face came into view. The target was irresistible. A hail of water bombs flew past him and into the house. Mr MacKay leapt backwards onto the floor. As fast as they could be made and filled, the missiles continued to fly and explode, soaking the inside of the house. The old folk by this time were at the end of their tether. The steady stream of sodden missiles went on and on while the brigands rendered a noisy new descant,

"We're aw throwin' bombs intae your hoose!"
"We're aw throwin' bombs intae your hoose!"

This went on until the stock of munitions dwindled and inevitably some windows were raised and neighbours began remonstrating with the small, well-organised army of toerags. True to their instincts, and fearing police intervention, Robert and his brother followed the other rascals as they all made off through the opposite backcourts into St George's Road. Robert felt only a tinge of shame to have been present during this inexcusable game perpetrated one hot summer day. Such feelings were transient for boys in Raglan Street. Mr and Mrs MacKay were known as grumpy old moaners. No neighbours actually came to their assistance during the half-hour when their lives had been made miserable.

Most of their pranks were never repeated. One was. It was Robert's own special game that took place regularly, but only on Saturdays.

War on windows

"Can ah get ma pocket money, Mammy? Ah've been good all week."

"Here you are, son. Don't spend it all on sweeties."

Jeanie gave him a sixpence and a ration coupon. He thanked her and made his way to Mary Began's sweetie shop to buy a bar of McCowan's Plain Highland Toffee. This cost him half his money. A chocolate-covered bar of toffee was an extra penny. This, he could not afford, because his next purchase needed the other half of his pocket money. To comply with his mother's light-hearted instructions, he was not buying more sweets. He was heading for W. Johnstone's ironmonger's shop in Garscube Road to spend the rest.

"Can ah have thruppence worth ae staples, please, mister?"

The shopkeeper carefully weighed the 'U' shaped staples, wound up a piece of newspaper into a cone, poured the nails in, and sealed it with a twist over the top. Robert held this gingerly, due to the sharp points sticking through the thin paper poke, and carefully manoeuvred it into his trouser pocket.

He had three elastic bands tied together. Fitted to a thumb and index finger, they made a sling to fire fairly safe paper pellets during war games. Robert's game on Saturdays was not so innocent. He was intending to use his metal staples instead of paper pellets. These metal missiles jagged his leg as he hurried down Raglan Street to his Auntie Lizzie's close. He was heading for his favourite firing range – the second-storey landing.

With all of his components in place, Robert settled down on his hunkers by the window overlooking the backcourt. A pane of glass was missing. He broke his bar of toffee into the eight pieces, and arranged them neatly in their paper on the stone floor. This was the private prelude to his Saturday morning mischief. A furtive glance over the sill allowed him to spy on the windows of the houses opposite – the

St George's Road tenements. When it was safe, he loaded a staple into his sling and fired it across the two backcourts. It pinged against a window. He ducked down out of sight. The first of eight bits of delicious toffee was placed in his mouth, and he sat back and sucked contentedly.

He stole another peek. A man was looking to see what had made the noise. When he retreated, Robert launched another staple at the window. This time, the window was flung open. The man leaned out to see who was playing games. Seeing nothing, he shook his head and slammed the window shut. Robert continued his war on various windows, causing maximum annoyance and consuming most of his stockpile of staples and his stash of toffee.

Eventually an irate man appeared and headed for the railings separating the two backcourts. If this man was to squeeze through the railing into the Raglan Street side, he could trap Robert on the stairs. The boy was cute enough to know that this would take time; just enough for him to execute his well-practised retreat – a quick sprint down the stairs and out into Raglan Street. Never even close to capture.

This solitary game had been invented by Robert and never shared with anyone. He was proud of his invention, his subterfuge, his concealment, and the fact that he never got caught. During its perpetration, he was thoughtless, nasty, cool, and calculating. He was a selfish little street urchin with no intention of sharing his game with anyone; or his bar of toffee, either. He knew all this was wrong, but it was fun to be so singularly full of mischief and very satisfying to so skilfully avoid capture.

His sister, Jean, met him at home. "Have you spent all your money, Robert?'

"Aye, the whole tanner."

"All on sweeties, I suppose?"

"No!"

"Well, what else did you buy?"

"Ginger," he lied.

Another clever escape, he thought, but sometimes he was too clever for his own good.

Catholic, Proddy, or pals

Robert was wandering home from school, feeling happy with himself. As he entered the bottom of Raglan Street, he spotted Davy the rag-store man, who gave him a wave, which was cheerfully returned. Ten paces later, a boy jumped out of a close right in front of him. Robert stopped dead. The boy stuck his face right up to Robert's and snarled at him,

"Are you a Catholic or a Proddy?"

This was a question with which Robert had never before been confronted. He was instantly afraid. The hairs on his neck stood on end. In the strange way of the human brain, this sudden terror caused it to work extremely fast. This challenging question was one to which he felt there were only two possible answers. It depended on which answer he gave whether there would be a fight or conciliation. His thoughts raced for a solution to solve this conundrum and survive. *What religion is he? Is it the same as mine? I need to think quickly, otherwise if I dither or show uncertainty, he's going to bash my face in any case. If I say Catholic and he's a Proddy...I get bashed. If I say Proddy and he's a Catholic...I get bashed. If only John was here. He would know what to do.*

In the microseconds it had taken to reach this stage, an answer popped into his brain. One that was so clever, he had to smile at its simplicity. The question posed was simply to establish if he was one or the other. This simple answer confirmed that he was one or the other. He responded to his aggressor's query with that word, fully expecting to see a puzzled look on his enemy's face. It would be in that moment he would saunter past the mystified numbskull.

"Yes!" he beamed.

There was no bewildered look, just a blinding flash in Robert's left eye when the hot-tempered inquisitor delivered a perfect right hook then rubbed his knuckles, turned, and ran away back into the close, loudly expressing his opinion of Robert's clever reply,

"That's whit ye get for being a smart bastard!"

Robert yelled after him, in an effort to sound dangerous, "You wait! Ma big brother's gonnae get you!"

He resolved that from then on he would try to refrain from such subtle diplomacy. He would simply knock the aggressor down before he had a chance to attack. He also resolved to find out from John how he could achieve that. His brother had a good laugh when he heard the story. He *was* impressed by the kid's clever gambit, but offered better advice: next time this happened, no matter *who* it was, "If he's in front of you, bang your knee intae his baws! He'll no be able tae hurt ye after that!"

Robert noted this good advice. He couldn't wait to try it. His chance came soon. In the school playground the following week, he was having a dispute with his pal, Ian Jardine. As the two vied for supremacy, holding each other by their jerseys, Ian found himself backed up against the wall. Robert held him there to stop him moving away. He pressed his body close up to Ian's and, taking his brother's advice, he raised his right knee with considerable force. Ian reacted as if he had been shot. Groaning horribly, he crumpled to the ground with both his hands clutching his middle.

Robert stood back, stunned by what he had done. His feelings for his erstwhile friend were confused: joy at winning the contest, but horror at having inflicted such obvious and extreme pain that rendered his pal completely helpless. He bent down with his hand on Ian's shoulder to show his remorse. "Ian, ah'm sorry! Are ye alright?"

In that strange and inexplicable way that boys have for forgiveness, Ian managed a reply. "It's okay, Roburt. Ma willie's sore but the pain's goin' away slowly. Where did you learn tae do that?"

"Ma big brother taught me."

His friend asked with a final grimace of pain and a semblance of a returning smile, "Gonnae no' dae it again?"

"Ah'll never dae that tae you again!" promised Robert

He helped Ian to his feet, and in minutes the two were off again to play. The strong bond with his pal was still intact. Just as well.

Slippery slope

Robert was proud of his new black boots. Jeanie hammered metal segs into them to prolong the life of the soles. She was not to know that these same metal studs would nearly end her son's life.

To enter the senior playground of Grove Street Primary School, the boys had to go down a sloping concrete ramp. Boots with segs meant you could slide down it with sparks flying off your feet. During the school dinner break, Robert was doing just that wearing his new 'tackety' boots. The ramp had grooves across to prevent slipping in icy weather. Sliding over them at speed made a noise like a machine-gun. Robert took his turn, but instead of turning sideways, he faced forward. His feet went faster than his body and he fell backwards, striking his head on the concrete. He lay motionless; out for the count.

His pal, Ian rushed to pick him up. "Roburt, are ye alright?"

There was no answer other than a groan. Ian called John Carly over for some help saying, "We'd better lift him up,

Carly. There's the bell. Get hold him and we'll take him tae the lines."

He heard none of this, but was vaguely aware of being lifted by his two classmates and marching with jelly legs into school where, at his desk, he promptly passed out again. He momentarily woke up to the sound of Miss McIntosh shouting at him, "Chessar! Wake up and pay attention!"

Bertie Crosshair was holding him in his place, but he immediately blacked out again. Thus, he spent the afternoon drifting in and out of consciousness. After school, his pals had a confab.

"How are we tae get him hame?" asked Bertie.

"One each side, take an arm each and we'll walk him up the road tae his close," said Ian Jardine.

"Ah'll walk behind in case he faws backwards," said Carly.

Robert's chums supported him all the way home, half-carrying and pulling him up six flights of stairs to his door. They had to get home, so they left him sitting on the landing to be found by his mother when she came home from work. Although he was still delirious, Robert picked up their last comments as the boys drifted away down the stairs.

Ian Jardine had a thought, "How come the teachers didnae try tae help? Robert could've been dyin'!"

"Jist shows ye," said Carly, "They couldnae give a fuck about us, could they?"

"Aye. You're right!" said Bertie "Hope he's awright, eh?"

Jeanie found her boy sleeping. She concluded he was dog-tired from playing, and put him to his bed. He recovered without any visible signs that he had been concussed. Next day his rescuers made sure he knew what had happened to him. They couldn't believe he had no memory of the fall or of the three of them bringing him home. In the weeks that followed, he had flashbacks of waking in the classrooms to teachers' stern rebukes. When he computed this with what his friends told him, he came to the same opinion as them about *some* teachers, but not *all* of them. *School was not all bad,* he thought, e*specially at the end-of-term parties.*

Bottle of ginger

On the last day of school before a holiday, parties were allowed in the classrooms. The school provided nothing. It was up to the parents to get their children a bottle of lemonade and a cake or a biscuit. An hour before the last bell, they got out their drinks and cakes under the direction of their teachers, who encouraged singing songs and telling stories. Robert made sure that his mother knew about the date of the party and that he needed to buy his supplies. Because she was away to work long before he got up, Jeanie gave him money the night before. He could buy his supplies from shops in a detour round to St George's Road on his way to school.

The next morning, he left the house nice and early to get to the baker's shop to buy his cake. It was safely wrapped in a brown paper poke in his school bag. He went into the shop next door for his lemonade. He looked up to the man behind the tall glass counter.

"A bottle o' ginger, please, mister."

The bottle was placed on the high counter. "That'll be a shilling, sonny."

"But ah've only got ninepence!"

"Well, a bottle of lemonade is a shilling, son. Do you not have enough?"

The boy responded by looking at the floor with shoulders drooping. "No, ah've only got ninepence."

How could this happen tae me? He thought. He was sure his mother would have given him the correct money, and was confused as to how he appeared to have been let down. He was also very worried about how it would look when he went into school without a bottle of lemonade! It would be horrible to sit there while all the others had theirs, and he would look very silly and, worse than that, very poor! His family's honour was at stake as well as his own sensitivity. He imagined how red his face would be when they all started to talk about how he was the only one whose mammy couldn't afford his bottle of lemonade.

Maybe it would be better not to go to school, he thought. He couldn't suffer the shame of turning up on the last day without the full complement of stuff for the party. Then he had an idea. He stepped back a pace so the man behind the counter could see his face clearly. His eyes filled with moisture as a prelude to tears. He rubbed one eye with the side of his hand, held the man's gaze, and in his weakest little voice pleaded with him, "This is for ma school party and if ah don't get a bottle o' lemonade they'll aw laugh at me. Ah canny go tae school without a bottle ae ginger."

"I'm really sorry, son," said the man. "I can't think how to get round your problem. Can you go home and get more money, perhaps?"

Robert answered, accentuating his hopeless tone, "No. My mammy's away tae her work."

His fears of going to the party without the bottle were growing. He felt the 'tear thing' would have got a better result. But his brain was still working overtime to solve this. *Ah've got it! There's thruppence deposit on each bottle, so in actual fact the lemonade only costs ninepence. Ah've got enough to buy the lemonade, but not the bottle*. It was worth a try!

He made an offer with his best innocent look and sweet little voice that only a man with a heart of stone could possibly refuse.

"Mister? If ah gave you ninepence for the lemonade and when ah've finished ma school party, ah bring back the bottle and no ask fur the thruppence, would that be ok?"

The shopkeeper had been watching the boy carefully. He was trying to assess the reliability of his plea and to weigh up the character of his persuasive customer. It may have been that he remembered his own schooldays and a party at the end of term. This may have prompted him to put himself in Robert's predicament and consider what he would have done in such a sorry fix. Whatever the reason, he evidently decided that Robert had scored highly with his ability to negotiate a fair offer that would solve the problem. In the end, if Robert came back with the empty bottle and waived the deposit, then no-one lost, everyone was a winner, what could be wrong with that?

"I like your style, son. Now, you give me the money for the lemonade. This bottle belongs to me. Put it in your schoolbag so it doesn't get broken. You have promised me you will bring it back, s, I expect you to be here after school. I hope you enjoy your party, now off you go and don't run."

"Thanks very much, mister. Ah promise tae bring it right back here after school. Cross ma heart an' hope tae die."

Robert was full of joy at having secured the article that would preserve his dignity and his family honour. He was not going to jeopardise that by making a false promise to this kind man. He left the shop and had a great time at his party. When school was over, he left the playground with the empty bottle held securely under his arm. Or so he thought! On the way up to Raglan Street, he broke into a run to cross North Woodside Road. The precious bottle slipped out of his grip and smashed to smithereens on the ground. He was distraught! He was on his way to repay the kindness of the nice man in the shop. Now he was in debt and had no way to repay it. There was only one way. He went home and had his tea and kept quiet about his bankrupt state.

Next morning, he woke early and tucked into his breakfast. It was Saturday, the first day of the school holidays.

He would carry on as if nothing had happened. Just like a normal Saturday.

"Can ah get ma pocket money, Mammy? Ah've been good all week."

"Here you are, son. Don't spend it all on sweeties."

He ran down the stairs and hurried round to the shop in St George's Road. When he entered, the man welcomed him warily. "Hello, sonny, I didn't expect to see you again."

"But ah made you a promise tae come back, mister!"

The shopkeeper smiled and nodded in agreement. He saw that Robert did not have the empty bottle but wanted to hear what this bright young entrepreneur was going to say. He thought, *this promises to be good; otherwise he would not have come back.*

"How was your party?"

"It was great, mister. Ah was bringing your empty bottle back yesterday after school, but it fell and broke. Ah've just got ma pocket money frae ma mammy and ah can pay you the thruppence for the bottle."

He handed over the silver sixpence and waited for his change. The shopkeeper took his coin and opened and shut the till. He reached over the counter and pressed Robert's change into his hand. He closed the boy's hand saying, "Hold that tight now and don't drop it. Off you go. Thanks for coming back."

"OK, mister. Thanks for the ginger. Cheerio!"

Outside the shop, Robert opened his hand. There, instead of a brass thruppenny bit, was his silver sixpence. He smiled, proud that his honesty had paid off. He fingered the three elastic bands in his trouser pocket. The decision was made. He headed for Mary Began's sweetie shop. Now he could have his McCowan's Plain Highland Toffee *and* his staples. On the way, he recalled his brother using a giant staple.

Poor cat!

A battle was raging in his Auntie Lizzie's backcourt. A dozen boys, including Robert and John, were fighting with elastic band slings and rolled-paper pellets. Their "ouches" and "oohjahs" reverberated off the walls. Robert's brother, John, suddenly yelled, "Hey! Look whit ah've found. It's a giant steeple."

It was about three inches long with two sharp ends. Danny looked at it and stated categorically, "John! You canny use that tae fire at us. A thing that size is bound tae kill somebody!"

"Don't be daft, you. Ah'll no hit anybody wae this. Ah'm gonny hit that cat."

A black cat just happened to be strolling along on the other side of the railings, evidently thinking the boys were not a threat. John inserted the staple into the sling and pulled the elastic out a little bit to tighten it without firing it. He invited the onlookers to decide, "Will ah shoot the cat?"

"John! Don't shoot it! You'll hurt it!" Robert pleaded.

"Naw ah'll no! Ah'll only hit it softly and it'll run away."

He pulled more on the elastic and launched the staple. What happened next had the whole gang transfixed, open-mouthed in astonishment, staring at the cat. It jumped up in the air but didn't run away. It landed in a crouched position and froze with fright. The staple had in some inexplicable twist of fate, turned round in the air so that both its pointed ends stuck into the side of the cat. It cried in a low *meow,* conveying a ghastly pain and a plea for help. It turned its head to look at the boys. Robert saw disappointment in its eyes. It seemed to be asking why these boys with whom it had no quarrel had inflicted such cruelty.

John was full of remorse. "Awwwhh naw!"

He vaulted the low railings, bent down and stroked the poor animal's head, trying to reassure the beast that he had not meant such a horrible result. The cat reacted by squatting down nearer to the ground with the elbows of its forelegs now higher than its back, its ears flattened, its tail jerking from side to side and its head turned away, seemingly to avoid the *next* attack. John continued to clap it in reassurance and murmured, "Ah'm sorry!"

The cat did not move. John eased his hand down and gripped the staple. With a quick jerk, it was removed. The animal winced and crouched lower with the sudden pain. It turned its head and looked at John as if to say, *do you expect me to be grateful?* Then it seemed to know that the silent boys wanted it to run away.

John stood up and moved away. The cat rose, still wary, and very slowly moved off to safety. The silence was broken by a shout from big Danny, "How the fuck could that happen?"

"That was a chance in a million. Ah didnae want tae hurt it, neither ah did," replied John sadly. "How dae you think ah feel? Ah've nearly killed a wee cat?"

"It was jist bad luck for the cat, John," said one of the lads. "It's got nine lives, so it's gonnae be awright. Don't worry about it."

"Aye, you're probably right," John agreed. "It'll maybe jist lick the two wee holes tae they get better."

He seemed to be comforting himself, but the incident had a strong effect on Robert's hero. The mystifying incident also left a marked impression on the other witnesses. They were bound to remember this for a long time after. Robert spoke to his brother.

"John, what are you gonny dae wae the staple?"

"See this big staple? It's goin' intae the midden. Ah'll never dae anything like that again!"

The gang had now lost all interest in firing pellets at each other. They drifted away to find some other, less harrowing activity. They went to watch the men that were gambling for money next to the air-raid shelters on the spare ground at the foot of the street.

Odds on

Robert was fascinated by this apparently simple game. A group of men, gullible punters, formed a circle. A man in the circle called the 'tosser' held two pennies on a flat stick in his right hand, with the palm upwards. He invited the onlookers to bet by shouting, "Heads-a-dollar!" This meant that the maximum stake was a dollar, or five shillings in British money. The watchers dropped their penny bets on the ground in front of them. The 'tosser' flung the coins spinning up into the air shouting, "Nae mair bets!"

If they landed as two heads, the assistant covered each bet on the ground with the same amount. The punters had doubled their money. The pennies could fall to the ground showing 'two heads', 'two tails', or 'a head and a tail'. Conversely, when the shout was "Tails a dollar!", those who bet on that would win if two tails came up. For obvious reasons there was never a shout of, "Heads and tails a dollar!" That could happen two ways, and the tosser was not stupid. The way they organised their game meant that each bet had three out of four ways for the punters to lose. They made a fortune from these simple hard-working folk. Gambling like this was illegal, mainly to protect the ordinary working man from shysters like these. Many a man lost his wage packet trying to win back his losses.

If the police were in the area, one of the lookouts gave a pre-arranged whistle and the shysters ran off with their bag of cash. The punters had to run or else be arrested and charged. The policemen collected the pennies still lying on the ground as 'evidence'. This 'evidence' was never reclaimed. Just another way the poor punters lost out. It was rare indeed to see such a thing as a friendly neighbourhood policeman round Raglan Street. They usually appeared during a gambling game or just after a gang fight had stopped. They were seldom seen when someone needed help. The cops were guardians of law and order, not a nursemaid service. It was up to the 'hoi polloi' to look out for each other.

Agony and angels

There were some really good people in and around Raglan Street. One came to Robert's aid when he was playing in the backcourt with some pals. He was wearing short trousers and ankle socks. On his feet were open-toed sandals with leather uppers and crepe soles. He was being chased at high speed down the derelict backcourt during a game of 'tig'. The shoes made a 'click-click' sound as his feet hit the ground. Suddenly his feet were making a 'click-clack, click-clack' sound. Three paces later, Robert fell to the ground yelling. He had trodden on a piece of wood with a nail sticking up. The nail went easily through the soft sole of his right sandal. The wood was now nailed to his foot.

He lay on the ground squirming with the pain. A woman appeared. She pulled hard on the wood. It split where the nail was and came away in her hand. Robert by now was lying with eyes screwed up in agony and sobbing sorely, the nail still holding his sandal onto his foot. She tried to keep him calm. "Hold on, wee man. Ah'll try and pull it out."

Robert yelled again as her fingers tried desperately to grip the small bit of the rusty wire nail that was barely showing through his sandal. She whispered to herself, "My God, it's stuck. It'll no' come out!"

With eyes full of tears, he turned to her and whimpered in pain, "Oh, missis, get it oot. It's awful sore."

The wretched woman looked helplessly at the youngster. Her maternal instinct was to save him even if it meant hurting herself, but what could she do? She was looking at the poor wee soul crying in anguish. This nail in his foot had likely gone into his bone. It was not for coming out. She said, "I need a pair of pliers."

In that moment came inspiration. She put her head down to the underside of Robert's shoe.

He felt a sharp pain and it was all over. This resourceful woman used her teeth like pliers round the nail. One swift jerk of her head and it was done. As she rose, Robert saw the nail in her teeth. It was covered in his blood. She spat it out, took off his sandal and sock, and inspected his foot.

Kneeling beside him on the ground, she looked into his face and whispered endearments, "There you are, wee fella. You've been brave. That must've been sore. Here, take your sock and your sandal and away ye go up tae your mammy and get your foot cleaned."

He remembered that face. She was not young. Nor was she pretty. Like a lot of women round where he lived, her face was full of lines. She smelled of cigarette smoke and drink. Her clothes were drab. She was not at all good to look at, appearing to be as hard as nails herself. Robert, however, saw a look in her face that she may not have shown for some time, being in such a sad condition. She looked at him and smiled. Her expression was of admiration for his bravery, but there was another significance in her gaze.

Robert saw a woman who looked like she had given up on life, but for that instant, helping a wee boy's pain, she was motherly and kind and felt good for it. They held eye contact for some seconds. He liked her. Suddenly, seemingly embarrassed with this closeness, she got up and was gone, hurrying away back to her own life.

As she walked away Robert said, "Thanks, missus!"

She never turned round; she just disappeared through the close. He didn't know her. Whoever she was, he would never forget her. She was his angel who smelled of whisky.

Sandshoe Sanny

There were very few angels round Robert's area. Some people could be classed as being between Joak Dan and the Devil. There was, for instance, Alex Purdon, the fourteen-year-old son of a man who owned a small shop in Lion Street. Boys from Raglan Street stayed clear of Lion Street and anybody who came from there. It was too dangerous even to go into their backcourt to get a ball back. Once over the wall, the ball was lost, along with the person going after it. Brick walls and washhouses separated the backcourts of the two streets.

The boy Purdon had only one leg. He wore a sandshoe on his one remaining foot, hence his nickname – *Sandshoe Sanny*. He was the object of scorn and derision, but only from a safe distance. The boy was ugly, having also lost one of his eyes. His use of an eye patch, a crutch, and an uncompromising look of hatred for humankind, made it wise to avoid him. He had an entourage of pals of the same ilk – dirty and belligerently hostile. They trotted after him like obedient little rodents, as he pivoted about on his crutch. His wild careering style of movement resembled Long John Silver from *Treasure Island*.

Robert's brother had come up against this rogue, and narrowly missed being beheaded by his flying crutch before shoving him on his arse and running away. He warned Robert to give a wide berth to Sandshoe Sanny Purdon. He was known to attack people for no reason other than for his own amusement – the hallmarks of a sadistic, psychopathic villain.

A fateful day arrived. Robert was standing on the flat roof of the midden, waiting his turn for a slide down the sloping roof of the washhouse. The trick was to sit on the stove-enamelled metal sheets covering the roof, slide down, and swing round the cast-iron vent stack that stuck up from the washhouse sink. From there, it was an easy 'shin' down to the backcourt and to climb back up onto the roof of the midden.

He noticed a movement on his left side. Turning round, he was stunned to see that Sanny Purdon and two pals from Lion Street had managed to climb up beside him. Sanny leant on his crutch, looking mean. Robert sensed the danger. He quickly glanced round looking for John, but he was alone. He looked into the hateful eye of his nemesis.

Purdon leered at him. On his ugly face was a smile that promised, *Ah'm gonny enjoy battering you!* He spoke, "Hullo there, Robert Chessnut!"

John's advice was ringing in Robert's ears; *attack is the best form of defence*. He spoke loudly and with as much confidence as he could, "You're not allowed on this dike. This is a Raglan Street dike, and youse better get aff it or ma big brother John's gonnae get youse."

He tried this brash ploy while casting another quick glance to locate John, but his brother was nowhere to be seen. Robert *was* frightened, but tried not to let it show. He noted that his pals on the washhouse roof had disappeared. Now he was totally alone. The last time he was like this, he got punched in the eye. His mind was again racing to find an escape from this bad spot. It was like a nightmare he had just woken from to find he was not dreaming. This was real!

"Your big brother's no' here! So ah can dae anything ah like, can't ah? Ah can dae you right now!"

He balanced precariously on one leg and poked the rubber-tipped end of his crutch into Robert's chest. It was clear that this ugly animal was going to do something very bad. Robert had to run or do something physical to Sandshoe Sanny. One idea was to take his brother's best advice and kick Purdon in the balls. The consequences of that could be quite serious. The midden roof was small. The odds were three-to-one in favour of the opposition. If Robert hit the one-legged, one-eyed wonder, he might just as well sign his own death warrant. Purdon's pals would toss him into the backcourt. Surely he would die from the fall or later from his injuries?

As Sanny moved to grab him, Robert decided that, rather than be thrown off, it was better to jump; it was only eight feet to the ground. He remembered being taught to drop from the pulley in Auntie Maggie's house when Bertie taught him how to be a paratrooper. The decision was as instant as the thought. He spun round on one leg to jump off, while shouting a loud expletive to his ugly foe, "You'll no' get me, Purdon, ye ugly basturd!"

In turning, Robert's right leg caught on something. He flew down off the midden and landed with a forward roll. Looking up, he saw Purdon staggering backwards, falling into Lion Street. Robert had unintentionally kicked away Purdon's crutch! He heard a plaintiff cry from over the wall, "Ya wee cunt, Chessar! Don't you worry, ah'll get you the *next time*!"

Robert's answer was pithy. "Well, ya fucker! Ah got you *this time*! Ah hope you broke your *other* leg!"

There may have been another riposte from Lion Street, but Robert was gone. Quick thinking had saved him this time. He thought it would be good to improve that skill. It made sense to be ahead of the opposition by thinking rather than fighting. All you had to do was reason it out. Doing that properly could very often get you out of trouble. It therefore followed that you could probably get away with anything if you were smart enough or cunning enough. But maybe he was becoming too cocky for his own good.

Grand larceny

He had some skill for deceit. He thought carefully before doing wrong for fear of being found out. In spite of his imagined propensity for self-preservation, this would-be Al Capone's judgement could be swayed by other inner feelings. He was just like most of his pals – selfish and greedy. Each Monday, Jeanie gave him three shillings and fourpence, which was his dinner ticket money for the school canteen. On the way to school, his pal Ian Jardine, made an attractive suggestion.

"What if we keep our dinner money? We can buy sweeties and stuff wae it."

Robert pondered this for a second before asking, "Whit if ma mammy finds out?"

"How'll she know?"

"She'll ask what we had for dinner."

"What's that got tae dae wae it?"

"Well. Ma mammy works in Partick where they cook the school dinners and she knows what's made every day."

"Well, we'll jist ask one o' the other boys when they come out, okay?"

"Aye, that seems awright."

So in they went to school, refrained from buying a dinner ticket, and between the two of them they pocketed six shillings and eightpence – a considerable sum of money for two young crooks. At dinnertime, they bought some sweeties and comics, frittering away some of their parents' hard-earned cash. They made sure to find out what food the canteen served.

Robert went home, confident of escape from detection when questioned. He need not have worried. His mother didn't ask him. The same drill was practised for Tuesday and Wednesday, and the master crooks encountered no problem. But something *was* wrong.

"Ian. Ah'm getting hungry."

"So am ah, Roburt."

Robert's mother was getting a little bit worried about a slight change in Robert's behaviour. He was normally a good eater. She knew that he was getting a three-course meal every day and usually, unless it was green spring cabbage, he reported that he had eaten all of it. She wondered why he was coming home and eating like a small horse. *Was he suddenly growing at a faster rate? Did he not like the food at school?* She was genuinely worried about her son's altered appetite. She decided to watch him closely the next night.

On Thursday, when he came in from school she said, "Hello, son. How was school today?"

"It was fine, Mammy. We had good games in the playground and Mr Sergeant told us his joke again."

"Did he? He's a nice man, Mr Sergeant. What was the joke he told?"

"If at first you don't succeed, suck sausages!" he said, and burst out laughing at the silliness of the joke. "It's no really funny, but it's the only joke he tells so it always makes us laugh."

Jeanie smiled broadly at the boy's happy state.

"Mammy, ah'm hungry. Whit's fur tea?" he asked unguardedly, flinging off his schoolbag and plunging into the chair by the fireplace.

"Something nice and I know you'll like it. It's macaroni and cheese."

"Oh great, ah love macaroni and cheese. Have you made a big lot?"

"Yes, son, and you can have as much as you like."

Robert by his time was completely relaxed by the fire, but he was about to be rudely awakened.

"What did you have for dinner today at school?" Jeanie asked.

He went rigid. He had made it to Thursday without being detected. He was not prepared for this test. He had not bothered to ask anyone what the school dinner was for that day.

"We had soup," he said, knowing that there was always soup.

Noticing his slight discomfort his mother asked, "What else?"

"Well. We had...savoury mince and totties," he tried hesitantly, with a slight questioning look.

"And what was for pudding?" she pursued.

"Well…it was semolina and jam," he offered.

Jeanie sat down in the armchair opposite and gave him a long look that showed she was a mixture of emotions. She looked unhappy, but at the same time angry and disappointed. With her hands folded on her lap she said, "We didn't make savoury mince today, son, and we didn't make semolina either. Have you been to the canteen this week?"

Robert took this information like a bullet to his brain. The game was up. The ball was up on the slates. He was for it, and no mistake. He had a pounding in his head that felt bad and he knew why. He realised also that he had been really bad to his mother, and had not properly thought about the hurt she would feel when she discovered what a rascal he was. He knew that he was a deceitful little brat and he was now thoroughly ashamed of himself.

"Mammy, ah'm sorry. Ah kept the dinner money and bought sweeties wae it." He blurted out. He began to sob through his welling tears, trying to stop them with his palms.

Jeanie looked at the urchin, seeing his wretched distress and heart-breaking remorse. Tenderly, she whispered to him, "Come , son. Give your mammy a cuddle. There now! Shh! There!"

He nestled to her, still shrugging his sobs. Jeanie continued her comforting. She was near to tears herself for her tormented son. She needed to reassure him that he had already punished himself. Now it was all over and in the past. He had learned his lesson the hard way. Stroking his tousled fair hair, she spoke softly. "I knew something was wrong. I was worried about why you were hungry. You've done a bad thing, but you've owned up and you've learned a lesson."

"Aye, Mammy, ah'll no dae that ever again. Honest, ah'm sorry. Ah'm sorry."

"I think you have punished yourself enough. You'll be hungry tomorrow, though."

"How, Mammy?" he asked, looking up at her from her lap.

"Well, you can't go to the canteen. You don't have a ticket."

"That's right," he said. "It serves me right for being bad, doesn't it?"

"Never you mind. I'll make you a playpiece, so my wee man won't starve."

"Mammy, ah'm sorry."

"I know. I know," she said. "But there's worse things happen in this world. Remember, if you want anything, you have to work for it. When you want something bad enough, you have to be patient and save up your pennies. Then you can buy it. Then it's yours to keep. You'll think more of it because you'll have earned it."

"Ah see that, Mammy. Ah really want tae get a bike and get you a fur coat. When ah grow up, ah'll get a good job wae lots of money. Then you'll see whit a good boy ah'll be. Ah promise!"

"Well. We'll see," said Jeanie.

She was pleased to hear it, but not convinced by his promise. She knew him better than he knew himself. *But you never know, maybe given time he will change. Was that not the way it was with mothers who love their sons? They make allowances for them, knowing how hard and unforgiving life can be.* She had no illusions about him having a bright future. It's not easy to progress in this world when you start from the back of the queue.

Jeanie's heart was sore thinking about her son's ambitions. She was getting nowhere with her own. Here she was, nearly forty-two and she couldn't even afford a bike for the boy never mind a fur coat for herself. Maybe one day, but it would be a long time coming. Her son, John, had gone on to the Woodside senior secondary school and was doing very well. Hetty had left her job in Boots the Chemist, having got a secretarial post with William Collins the book publishers. She was bringing in good money and helping so much with the boys and the rest of the chores of the household. Jeanie was, however, having problems with her other daughter. Jean was finding it hard to keep a job.

But, thought Jeanie, *she was trying her best. Isn't that all you can expect from your kids?*

Late riser

Robert's two sisters were completely different from each other. Hetty was dedicated to looking after the family and the house. She had a good job, and able to bring in some money to help her mother feed the five of them. Jean, on the other hand, tried so many jobs. It wasn't long before she would fall out with her boss and either get sacked or just walk out in a fit of bad temper. Although she did bring in some money, it was Hetty and her mother between them who kept the wolf from the door.

Hetty was houseproud. This was not a bad thing, as long as the rest of the family stayed out of the way when she was cleaning. On Saturdays, Robert and John were given two jam jars and sent to the pictures. Not all of the cinemas took them, but the Astoria did. Hetty sometimes took a turn as cashier there, and took jam jars in exchange for tickets. The boys came home one Saturday after the film show. Hetty had washed the linoleum floor covering in the kitchen, and had put down newspapers to help it to dry. As they entered, they always got the same shout from their big sister, "Don't stand on the floor!"

"OK, Hetty, we'll jist walk round the walls."

"Don't be cheeky, you two. Stand on the newspapers."

She was a hard worker and very bossy, but she was a real asset to the family, well liked and respected by her wee brothers. Her younger sister, Jean, however, did not show this level of respect. She thought that life should be easier. Hetty just made things unbearable by persistently cleaning and tidying. She strongly disliked Hetty's dictatorial attitude.

Robert watched as things came to a head one day. Hetty was brushing the floor of the kitchen, while Jean was lazing in

156

the fold-down bed-settee in the recess. Normally this would have been folded up out of the way, but Jean had been out late the night before. She was still in bed at ten in the morning! This was not pleasing Hetty.

"Jean! You'll have to get up. I have to clean this floor."

"Can you no' leave it till later? Ah jist want a long lie. Ah was out late last night."

"No! It's not my fault you were out gallivanting all night. I need to get this done. Now, get out of your pit and let me get on!"

"Ah'm not getting up. Ah'm too tired."

"Well, I don't know how you can be tired. You never do any work!"

"We're no' aw like you, Hetty-house-proud. Leave me alone, 'Lady Muck!' Ah just want a wee lie-in."

With that parting shot, Jean made lazy yawning noises and pulled the blankets over her head. Hetty took decisive action. With a deft movement of her foot, she lifted the bed end frame, intending only to raise it enough to sweep underneath. At least, the watching boy *thought* that was her intention. Unfortunately, she lifted it too much. With loud twangs and squeaks, the whole bed closed up, completely engulfing Jean!

Hetty simply carried on with her cleaning and said, "Oh well! *Now* you can have a long lie-in!"

Muffled sounds came from inside the couch, while Hetty calmly cleaned the rest of the floor. Robert was on the chair by the fire, helpless with laughter. Jean promised to get up. Hetty freed her. This only happened once! When Jean emerged from the sofa, Robert made for the door. At times like that, it was safer for a youngster to be out on the street.

Robert aged 12, ready for the sword dance at QVS.

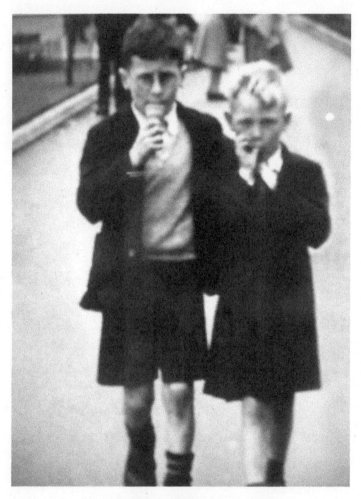

Robert with his big brother, John

Robert at the age of two

Statue of George and the Dragon at
St Georges cross, Glasgow

The bridge at the top of Baird's Brae,
starting point of all the adventures at the canal

Robert aged ten at his sister Hetty's wedding 1950

The canal bridge where skinny dipping took place on summer nights

Primary school photograph 1950 with
Robert fourth from right on back row

Robert's 'mammy', Wee Jeanie,
making a cup of tea in Raglan Street

Robert and his South African Table Bay Sherry bottle
complete with dummy teat

Aerial view of Cowcaddens in the late fifties. Three streets
make an "H" shape with .Raglan Street to the left,
St Georges Road to the right and Braco Street
joining them. Number 27 Raglan Street is on the left
side facing the ruined church on the spare ground where
Lyon Street tenements used to stand

Robert, standing second from right,and some of his
first XV rugby team prior to leaving QV School in 1959

SEVEN
1950

When Robert went out to play in Raglan Street, he was rarely on his own. Mostly, there was something going on, games to be played, dikes to be climbed, ropes to be skipped, or a peever to be pushed. Occasionally, there were bigger and bolder adventures to be had. Some of these were of questionable morality, dubious honesty, tarnished honour, or utter mental dejection. Because of this, some had short-lived appeal whilst others generated lasting self-reproach.

Leona Satorelli, through the curtains

Some people get uptight about how children should be shielded from the more exotic aspects of adult life. In some ways, they miss the point. Youngsters, out of curiosity, will find these things out for themselves in various unsanctioned ways. During this learning process, Robert was very rarely shocked by what he saw or heard or read. In most cases, a well-adjusted youngster will benefit from instructions received from a responsible adult, such as their teacher or parent. There are, however, many unofficial sources of edification.

There was a ground-floor house at the foot of Raglan Street, the back window of which was quite high up from the backcourt, making the room inside relatively discrete. To see inside, it was necessary to climb up onto the outside windowsill or stand on somebody's shoulders. Who would want to spend time and effort to spy through the window? In this house, however, there seemed to be a good reason to spy. The curtains were always drawn…even during the day. A girl called Leona Satorelli and her mother lived there. What they got up to in there was the object of much speculation amongst the boys of the street.

"They probably work on the nightshift and sleep aw day," said Big Danny.

"Don't be daft, Danny. Women don't work at night. Ah think they've got a German prisoner of war in there and don't want tae give him up," said Danny's brother.

"Don't talk shite, Bobby. The war's finished long ago!" scoffed Danny

"Well, how is it we never see anybody coming out during the day? The door opens and shuts but naebody comes out. Answer me that, Danny."

"It's because somebody's goin' in."

"That's daft as well," said Bobby. "If people are goin' in and naebody's comin' out, the place must be full up."

"Mibbe they're goin' oot the windae, Bobby, intae the street?"

The speculation was going nowhere. It was causing some mirth but not leading to any sensible conclusion; quite the reverse. They just got more curious to discover the answer to the mystery. It was agreed that one of them was going to have to look in the window. When darkness came, Robert went with four boys with a scheme for one of them to climb up to the window.

The honour fell to Archie Carbide, who peeped through a chink in the curtains. Those holding him in his precarious perch were in for a shock.

"Ah can see a man wae nae claes on! There's a wummin the same! They're on the bed, actin' like two dugs!" whispered the astonished boy,

"Come down, Archie. Let me see!" demanded Billy.

One by one, with much soft-spoken cajoling, they took turns to balance on the sill to peep through the curtain. In the space of two or three minutes, they got a precise pictorial sex education. The news of this juicy new discovery spread quickly, but only amongst the boys in the street. This was one of their many well-kept secrets. It mattered little that the ladies of the house were only earning some money in order to live. The boys seemed to accept this without judgement. They gave no trouble to the participants. What would be the point of causing trouble, only to spoil a free show for the careful voyeurs? Thus, the privacy of the two women was maintained, as well as some local men. The novelty for this small group, as usual, soon passed and other curiosities beckoned.

Bertie Kroam's bike

Up Baird's Brae and to the left, there is long, slow-curving stretch of the canal overlooking Firhill football ground. Folk

169

could stand and steal a free look at the Partick Thistle matches or the dog racing. In the summertime, open-air swimming was popular in the wide part of the canal between Firhill stadium and Baird's Brae. There were no buildings to block the sunshine. The canal bank was broad and safe for spectators, and for young lasses to guard the clothes of their heroes showing off in the water.

Nearby, Robert and his pals had gone fishing. The day was hot and sunny, ideal for swimmers and fishermen. The boys were not hoping to catch fish. They were after a much more valuable harvest. Using pieces of rope with makeshift metal grappling hooks tied on the end, they were hoping to recover anything usable from the murky depths of the canal. Most things dredged up were thrown back. A tight rope raised expectation of some marvellous treasure being hauled up. Anything made of metal would be sold in a scrapyard. The canal bank soon became littered with piles of free booty.

"Look! Ah've got something!" shouted Bertie.

"Whit is it?" said Archie, turning to see the new catch.

"It's a pair o' handlebars, but it's heavy! Ah think they're caught on something!"

"Can ah help ye?" offered Robert, rushing over, eager to see the new prize.

"Naw! Ah'll dae it! Ah think ah've got a whole bike, look! There's a front wheel and a frame comin' up. Aye! It's a whole bike. Archie, Robert, give us a hand to pull it out!"

Bertie Kroam had hooked a bicycle that seemed to be intact. This was a real prize for the lucky boy. To find a whole bike, no matter in what condition, was like striking gold! It was covered with slime, but its new owner was overjoyed.

"This is a fuckin' cracker! Ah'm takin' this hame right away tae dae it up."

Archie Carbide disagreed. "It's covered in green slippy slime, Bertie!"

"Ah know, but ah'll soon clean it up. It's a brammer, intit, Archie?"

"Aye! You're dead lucky, so ye are. Gonny give us a shot on it once ye get it fixed, Bertie?"

"Aye, nae bother, if you give us a hand tae clean it up. When we get it goin', we'll share it! Only you and me and Robert, though, the rest'll huv tae hire theirs!"

"Jist think, Bertie. We'll be able tae play on it aw day. Where are ye gonny keep it?"

"Up the stairs on the landing."

"On the landing? It'll get knocked! How no' keep it in the washhouse? Then ye can lock it in an' naebody'll knock it?" suggested Robert.

"Naw, ah'll keep it on the stair and take aff the front wheel. Naebody's gonnae steel a one-wheel bike, ur they, Archie?"

"Somebody wae one wheel might knock it!" Archie screeched, laughing as usual at his own joke.

"Oh! Ah' didnae think o' that," mused Bertie. "Well, ah'll just take the two wheels aff! Naebody's gonny steal a bike wae nae wheels, are they?"

Rising to the occasion with a new, hilarious observation, Archie made the ultimate suggestion. "How no' take aff the frame, saddle, an' peddles as well, Bertie? Naebody's gonny knock a bike that's no' there, are they?"

Archie screamed, laughing and writhing in pain at his contemptible humour, while Robert and the rest of the jesters gathered round to share the fun.

Bertie spat back with venom, "Very fuckin' funny, ya wee basturd! You're no getting a share o' ma bike now. Ah'll fix it masel, so you can jist fuck aff!"

With a display of genuine remorse in an attempt to re-cement the recently-formed treaty, now seemingly irretrievably broken, Archie pleaded, "Aw, Bertie, ah was only kidding. Don't go aff the heid. Ah'll help you wae it and the two o' us 'll get it goin'!"

"Here!" retorted his late pal. "You kin have the rope and the hook. See if you can catch one o' your own. An' when ye dae, don't come tae me lookin' for a hand tae dae it up, because Robert and me 'll be too busy doin' mine up! Cheerio!"

He trundled his heavy, slimy bike away over the cobbles, heading for home. How he was going to repair the bicycle without having any money did not occur to him. All he knew was he had something of considerable value over the rest.

It was to prove a brief luxury. The rest, who witnessed Bertie and Archie's dramatic verbal altercation, were not the least bit phased by it. It was quite normal for such alliances to be formed and shattered again in an instant when protagonists like these kids were bereft of possessions of any value. The truth is, if anyone had more than his pals, they banded together to ridicule the more fortunate one and he became an outcast of the troupe for a time. So it was with Bertie as he strode away with his trophy towards Baird's Brae. Without him hearing, a discussion took place amongst the now underprivileged bunch, concerning the state of Bertie's new vehicle. Presently a cheerful laugh went up.

Just as Bertie was reaching the top of the hill and achieving safe departure from his pals, the cruel choir chorused, "Hey! Bertie! Your tyres are flat and you've no' got a saddle! You're gonny get a sore arse ridin' your bike. Ha! Ha! Ha! Ha!"

Bertie hurried away down the hill with tears tickling his face. He did not like what had happened. He felt the cold chill of being isolated. Hearing that scornful laughter, he wanted to put as much distance as possible between himself and them.

Later that evening, Bertie went back up to the canal with his pal Robert. They were pushing a green bicycle. The algae had dried hard, giving it the appearance of a green Vindec – the best bicycle in the hire shop; but only from a distance. Bertie rolled the dilapidated contraption into the water. As it disappeared, he turned away with his head bowed. He flung his arm around Robert's shoulder and headed back with him towards Baird's Brae. The dream of owning a bike was shattered. An emptiness that he found hard to bear entered his sore young heart. Two passing adults saw him disposing of his dirty bike.

"These kids today! Imagine throwing a good bicycle into the canal like that. Somebody should do something about it! That bike could have gone to someone who would appreciate it!"

Their cruel social comment was whispered loud enough for Robert and Bertie to hear the unjust criticism. Though it hurt, the irony was lost on the two boys. Robert tried to cheer his pal with a prediction.

"Never mind them, Bertie. Someday you and me'll get bikes."

"Aye, someday, Robert, but by then ah'll be auld."

Robert was not so sure. All they needed was enough money. Robert thought a wee business would be a way to make some. If only he had the brains to get one going.

Sticks

Someone he was close to had brains – his brother John. When they were getting into their beds that night, Robert put his business thoughts to his mentor. "John, can ah ask you something?"

"Aye, whit is it?"

"See if ye start a business, can ye make a lot o' money?"

"It depends on the business. Some need a lot o' money just tae get started."

"Can you no' start one without any money? Like finding things and then selling them?"

"I think you would have tae know what people wanted. Ah suppose if you find something that folk need every day and ye sell it tae them cheaper than the shops, then you could make a bit o' cash. Can you think o' anything like that, Robert?"

"Aye, they need messages like bread and milk and stuff like that. Is that any good? Ah could charge them for running tae get them."

"Well, that's no' a bad idea, but dae ye no' think it might be better if we made something. Then we could sell it and it would make a good profit. Let me think aboot it and see if ah come up wae anything."

Next morning, John got up and came through to the kitchen. Robert had placed 'spools' of newspaper and kindling wood in the grate. All John could see were two wee legs sticking out of the bunker. He was getting a shovel-full of coal to put on the fire.

Robert's head appeared just as John shouted, "Robert! You're a wee genius!"

"How, John?"

"Sticks! That's whit we'll sell. Sticks for the fire! Robert! We're in business!"

Everyone's house needed paper and sticks for lighting the fire. Paper was in abundance in the middens. Wood was not. Easy! Kindling was sold in the shops in small bundles. It was relatively expensive. If John could find a source of cheap (or free) wood, they could get started.

He was not long in organising the usual gang to go round the grocer shops begging for unwanted wooden boxes. The youngsters were told to smile nicely to get as many free boxes as possible. The older boys worked with borrowed hatchets in Auntie Maggie's backcourt, and a production line was formed to chop boxes into piles of kindling. The middens were raked for paper and anything made of wood. Tomato baskets, made of thin strips of wood and having round metal handles across the middle, were ideal containers for presenting the kindling to their customers. Customers paid a deposit for each box and got it back when the boys came with the next load a few days later. The clients usually waived the deposit. They were delighted with the service and appearance of these enterprising young 'businessmen'. Each package was a bargain, holding twice as much as the shops gave. There were two salesmen: John and Big Danny. They selected only two assistants. The four of them transported the merchandise in two homemade wheelbarrows to customers in the bigger tenement houses around Maryhill Road. John and Big Danny went to the doors, and handled the money. They noted their best customers and soon had a regular clientele.

At the end of the day's trading, 'wages' were awarded according to the effort and age of the employees. All who took part in the business got paid. These workers had no idea how much money was being turned over; they were just happy to get a few coppers for sweeties. It was not unusual on a Saturday to sell twenty boxes of sticks for a shilling each.

Robert's big brother was the managing director. For some reason, Robert always got sixpence. Nepotism was fine by him. This small business carried on for a long time without the shops knowing. The only drawback was the supply of wood. If the shops had none to give, it meant the business had to stay small on the basis of availability of raw materials. Still, it proved quite a little earner for John and Big Danny. It wasn't long before John had come up with another scheme. With this one, he had none of the heavy work, just the brainwork. He sold the franchise for sticks to Big Danny. With his carefully saved profits, he decided to employ sub-contractors for his next clever little business. It was to prove very profitable but, like the sticks, only for a while.

Beer bottles

Children were not allowed to enter the public bars. If it were necessary to contact an errant father, a boy who was sent to the pub to hunt him down could do one of two things. He could go to the pub door, pull it open a little bit, and try to attract his daddy. The other was to enter the 'family' room to ask the bartenders to tell his father to get home. This family room facility was also for returning empty beer bottles for the thruppenny deposit.

John spotted this as a good source of free cash. He decided to turn it into an organised business, along the lines of selling firewood. He got a group together to go round doors to beg for any empty beer bottles. Some folk were too lazy to return them to the pub. As usual, the middens got raked for bottles. On a Saturday it was not unusual for five or six helpers to amass thirty to forty bottles. John paid a penny for each one. He took them to the pub and got more than five shillings for five minutes' work. The best-laid schemes, however, don't always go smoothly. John had operated this system for a number of Saturdays and was again in the family room at Roper's Public Bar with his stock of bottles.

"Here's some mair bottles, mister."

"Right, son. I can take this one, this one, and these two. The rest aren't ours."

"What dae ye mean, they're no' yours?"

"Well, they havnae got our stamp on them. See the letter 'R' stamped in red on the label?"

"But ah've always gave you ma bottles."

"That's the problem, son. We've been getting more bottles in than we gave out, so they must be from other pubs. Sorry, son, it's the bosses' idea."

This was bad news. He had laid out some cash for these. This sudden loss of funds and income could spell the end of John's well-organised little group. He went home to consider his options. All the other local pubs refused to pay boys for returning these bottles. This was a breach of contract with the buyers of the bottles who had paid the extra to get the beer in the first place. John preferred not to take the matter to court. He preferred to take their bottles to the one pub that had never complained and paid up every time, namely Roper's Bar. Up till then, his scheme had worked. Clearly, another plan was required. John considered this situation for a few days. Then, with another flash of inspiration, he went out and called the partners to a board meeting in the washhouse. He told them the news about Roper's new rules but insisted it was not all bad. One boy disagreed.

"It's nae use, John. If they don't take our bottles, we're fucked!"

"Naw we're no'. It's actually better for us. Roper's have done us a favour. They canny refuse any bottle wae a rid stamp on it."

"Aye, John, bit whit aboot the ones wae nae stamp?"

"Easy! We'll put an 'R' on every bottle we find."

"How're we gonny dae that?"

"Ah'll make a stamp and get some rid ink."

"Hey, John, you're a genius!" said Big Danny.

"Naw ah'm no. Ah'm just brainier than *you*. Ah'll show youse the morra."

He searched the house for a rubber stopper. With a pair of pliers, he held a nail over the gas cooker flame till it was red-hot. Using that and a razor blade, he managed to make a

decent replica of Roper's identification stamp. A bottle of
cochineal from the cupboard would do for crimson red.
After a few attempts with an ink-soaked rag, he reproduced
a good clean print on a bit of newspaper. He then tried the
forged stamp on a beer bottle label. He smiled, *that is really
very nice. If ah didnae know it wiz fake, it would fool me.*

Now he had to put it to the test. Next day, he went to the pub
to hand over the bottle. He didn't recognise the barman, so
he adopted a confident but nonchalant attitude as he offered
his masterpiece.

"Here's one ae your bottles, mister. Can ah get the deposit?"

"Right, son,"

John watched for any sign of suspicion on the barman's face as
he inspected the label. There was a slight flicker. The barman
did a double take on the label. *Oh-oh!* thought the boy, *this
could be awkward.* But he stood his ground. The man turned
round to attract the attention of the other barman.

"Hey, Wullie! Is this ours?"

At this sudden change in the usual calm behaviour, John
began to sidle very slowly towards the door. Wullie
sauntered over to his mate and said, "Whit's the problem,
Jim?"

The future of John's new business hung precariously. All
depended on the next sentence.

"Dae we sell Fowler's strong ale?"

John totally relaxed, *Thank fuck! Ah thought it wiz the stamp.* He knew now that the other barman's reply would win him his three pennies.

"Aye, dopey, that's ours. We've sold that here for the last hunner year. Gie the wean his thruppence."

John put out the good news to the local bottle gatherers. There followed a stream of bottles from everywhere, as boys from all around brought theirs to be stamped by the forger. John's new business tactic was to sell the stamping service for a fee of one penny per bottle. This was his *easy* way to riches, because there was no need then for him to take the bottles to the pub; others were doing all of the work, and his business was booming. This may have been the first case of sub-contractors being employed by a boy in the street. John knew it couldn't last forever: *the guys in the pub are gonny notice that they're getting full up wae bottles again.*

Of course, he was spot on. Within a few weeks, Roper's bar manager realised what was going on. He lifted his eyes to the ceiling and swore.

"They clever wee bastards! They've made their ain stamp for the bottles. That's how we're getting more than we did before the stamp wiz used. Right! Change the stamp, and next week don't take any with the 'R' stamp."

A week later, the boys who took their bottles to Roper's bar were told that they had been found out. They were not getting their three pennies. They had also paid a penny to John for the old 'R' stamp. He got no more requests for his stamping service. The bottom had fallen out of the market.

Some businesses just cannot be sustained! The goose with the golden eggs had been killed. John closed down the business, but it wasn't bankrupt! John was the one with the eggs. He had saved a tidy sum from this and selling the sticks business. His secret money box below the bed held a goodly hoard. He decided to use a chunk of this to give his youngster an adventure he would love.

Epic journey

Being only thirteen, John had to seek permission from Jeanie before embarking on this special treat with his young brother. Robert was unaware of John's good intention. He came in from playing to hear the end of what had been a longer conversation.

"We'll go early on Saturday and be back in time for dinner. It should be probably about five or six, Ma."

Jeanie was not enthusiastic, but was reluctant to stand in the way of this honest escapade. She sensed danger in John's proposal, but he was sensible and resourceful. It would be wrong of her to deny him the pleasure of giving Robert a great day out.

"Alright, son, but make sure the pair of you don't get lost or get hurt. Robert, you make sure you do everything John tells you. I'm going down to see Lizzie just now, so you can tell Robert what your plan is."

Robert was becoming increasingly puzzled. As Jeanie left, he turned to his brother, "John, what were you and Mammy talking about?"

"OK, Robert. You're always complaining about hiring bikes for jist an hour at a time? Well, ah'm hiring bikes for a whole day. You and me are goin' for a run tae Loch Lomond."

"But, John, that's ten bob, and Loch Lomond must be a hunner miles away!"

"It's awright, Robert, ah've got the money saved up and it's only aboot eighteen miles to Balloch. We kin get there in a couple o' hours, get something tae eat and drink there, and be back in time for dinner. You'll manage that nae bother!"

"Aye, that sounds great if we get good bikes. When are we goin'?"

"We'll get two bikes hired early on Saturday mornin' and set aff right away."

Saturday found them outside the shop in Cedar Street waiting for it to open. They would have the best choice of bikes. They were unhappy to discover someone had bent the green Vindec, so it was out of commission. The owner helped them select two that were apparently in good working order.

John told the man, "Ma wee brother an' me are gaun a long run. Ah want tae be sure the bikes are no' gonny break down after a few miles."

"Where are you two going?" he asked.

"We're gaun tae Loch Lomond. So we need good bikes."

"That's some journey for two wee boys. Are you sure you can do it and get back again?" The man sounded sceptical.

"Nae bother!" said John. "If ma wee brother can dae it then so can ah!"

Robert, who had no idea where Loch Lomond was, piped up, "Ah've never been tae Loch Lomond, mister. Ah'll be okay wae ma big brother!"

The man looked at Robert with some sympathy. "Oh well, if you say so."

Jeanie made some jam and cheese sandwiches for them. These were stuffed inside John's jersey, which was tucked into his short trousers. Thus prepared, they set off down North Woodside Road to Great Western Road.

"Robert, ah know Great Western Road leads aw the way tae Loch Lomond. Aw we huv tae dae is follow the road tae Balloch, and Loch Lomond is about a mile frae there. You keep up wae me, and if ah'm goin' too fast just shout me back. OK?"

His charge was quite happy with that. They made good progress along the main road, staying close to the edge of the pavement. To attempt this journey could be said to be foolhardy. Like any escapade by these two youngsters, it was fraught with all sorts of perils. Sure, they could get lost or knocked down by fast cars on the way. But they were confident and lucky. As far as John was concerned, there were more risks in some of the events they took part in and around in Raglan Street.

They pedalled steadily along the road past Bingham's Pond. This was a well-known landmark, only a penny tram ride from St George's Cross. Summers were spent here fishing for baggy minnows; winters spent sliding on the ice. Anniesland Cross was negotiated safely, and the road from there was dual carriageway through Knightswood, Duntocher, and on past Bowling, where the traffic was fastest. They had been cycling non-stop now for about two hours and were well past Alexandria, shortly reaching Balloch.

"This bike o' mine's getting a bit hard tae pedal, Robert. Loch Lomond is only a wee bit further. It's a flat road now all the way tae the loch, so we'll just keep goin' tae we get there," said John.

Robert was following his brother closely on the last bit of road just before the lochside when he noticed John slowing down. He had slowed to a crawl. His brother stopped without putting his foot down, and just fell to the left onto the grassy bank at the side of the road with his feet still on the pedals and him still sitting on the bike.

"John! What's the matter! Are you awright?"

John spoke through clenched teeth. "It's ma legs. They've jist seized up wae this bike. The pedals willnae go round an' ah canny go any further! So we'll jist have our picnic here. OK, Robert?"

Upset to see his heroic brother in such a state, Robert jumped off his bike and ran to help disentangle him from his machine. John lay back on the grass to ease his aching legs. After they had eaten their sandwiches, John assessed the bike. He found that the front and back wheels were running freely. The problem had to be the spindle through the pedals. The bearings must have run dry.

John had given up peddling through sheer exhaustion. He had done eighteen miles on this supposedly 'good' bike. He was not happy. There was nothing for it but to walk back to Glasgow. The prospect of that didn't bother John, but he was concerned for his little brother. He told Robert the problem and showed him the sticky pedals. Robert suggested that they maybe needed some oil. He knew something about bikes. John agreed that was a good idea but thought, *where are we gonny get some oil?*

"I know! C'mon, Robert, there's a garage up the road in Balloch. We'll ask the man there if he'll help us."

They pushed their bikes back up the hill to the garage. John told the mechanic of how their epic journey has come to a sticky end. The chap was impressed. Ten minutes later, he had the stiff pedals released and working fine. He gave them each a small bottle of lemonade and waved them goodbye. Off they went to retrace their eighteen hard miles back to Glasgow. Their journey to Balloch had taken them less than three hours. Seven hours after leaving the hire shop, they carried the bikes up to their house in Raglan Street. Over tea, they told Jeanie of their grand adventure.

On Sunday morning, they told the story, with some embellishments, to the bike shop owner. He was glad the boys had got there and back safely and made his apology to John. He assured him he could have any bike he wanted for the next five hires, free of charge. This was his way of repaying him without passing any money over. He expected John would be very pleased to have such a good deal.

He was wrong. John was a good negotiator. "Whit about ma wee brother? He was wae me! It was his idea tae get oil fur the pedals or ah would've thrown the bike away!"

The man was unmoved by the strong argument and said so. "I'm sorry, John, but the bike's your responsibility. It was your idea to go and see Loch Lomond, not mine. If the bike had seized up in Raglan Street, it would have been nae bother tae get it back tae this shop. Ah've made you a good offer. Take it or leave it. It's aw the same tae me, son."

John was not to be put off. He rounded on the man. "Listen, mister; Ah spent ten bob getting these bikes off you to take ma wee brother to see Loch Lomond. Because your bike wisnae up tae it, my wee brother didnae even get tae *see* Loch Lomond. You spoiled ma chance to gie him a big surprise day out. An' another thing as well…ah know most o' the boys that hire bikes frae you. If you don't sort this out for me and ma brother, you might find you lose a load o' customers! There's another bike shop in North Woodside Road, you know?"

This cogent reminder of the need to retain the goodwill of his clients had a remarkable effect on the shop owner. It was bad enough having to compete with the other shop, without the added cash-flow problem of a boycott by the Raglan Street bunch. He relented.

"Listen! I'm sorry you missed the best part of your day with the wee boy. I'll make it up tae you and your brother. I'll give youse both a bike each day next week free for an hour, OK, Johnny?"

"Aye, that's fine wae me, but ah want the green Vindec," said John.

"Whit about you, Bobby?" he asked Robert.

"Ma name's no' Bobby, it's Robert."

"Oh sorry, Robert. I'll remember in future."

"Ah want the green Vindec as well."

"You two boys 'll ruin me, dae ye know that? See you next week."

They returned home to Raglan Street. To have had undertaken an epic journey successfully and negotiated a great deal for free bikes over the next week gave John an immense feeling of satisfaction. It certainly increased his standing with his kid brother. Robert still held a strong yearning for *his own* bike one day. Until then, any means of transport would suit him rather than having to walk in the rain.

Why walk?

He was in the Kelvingrove Park one Sunday with his pals, Ian Jardine and Bertie Crosshair. When they set out, the weather had been promising a day of sunshine. Now, on their way home, they were miserable and getting soaked in a heavy summer rainstorm. They took the shortest way back through Princes Street, past many parked cars. As they scurried along with heads down to minimise the rain on their faces, Jardine complained, "This is pish, this rain! Ah'm freezin'!"

Crosshair shouted, "If only we could get intae a motor, then we'd be out o' the rain."

That's when Jardine had a brainwave. "How can we no' jist get intae a motor and drive home in it?"

"Very funny!" said Bertie. "You canny drive, Ian. Can you, Robert?"

"Ah don't know, but ah'll try it. Ah think you pull a knob and it starts. Then ye jist turn the steering wheel and it's dead easy."

After trying some car doors, they eventually found one unlocked. In seconds, the three were inside, with Robert in the driver's seat. The rain was pelting down and the noise was like being inside a drum, but they were happy to be out of the downpour. Robert scanned the words on the switches and knobs.

"This wan says *starter* on it. Should ah pull it an' see if it works?"

The other two agreed. Robert pulled the knob. The starting motor made the *rruummph-a-rruummph-a-rruummph* noise, turning the engine. Robert held the knob for a couple of seconds and then let go.

"It disnae want tae start. How can ah drive it if it disnae start?" he grumbled.

"Try again," the pals suggested.

This had the same result. The car was not going to start. They didn't know it needed an ignition key. Maybe it was just as well. It was also fortunate that it was in neutral, or else pulling the starter would have sent it lurching into the car in front or the one behind. By this time, the trio were totally puzzled. Eventually the battery wheezed its last. Pulling the starter knob produced nothing!

The boys got out and banged the doors in disgust. The rain had abated. They set off again, three abreast, along the pavement. A sudden shout from behind them made them stop and turn round. They saw an elderly man coming awkwardly towards them waving a walking stick. He shouted again, "Hey! You boys! Come back here! I want a word with you!"

There was no need for further discussion; they took to their heels and shot away, stopping only when they reached Great Western Road. A quick look back assured them that they had outrun their pursuer. They saw him standing waving his stick at them, but they were now too far away to hear his angry yells.

Ian gave his opinion. "Dae ye think he's a bit annoyed, Robert?"

"Aye! He's nae right tae complain. Ah don't think it wiz his motor."

"Roburt!" said Bertie. "See the next time you pick a motor, gonny get wan that works?"

They all giggled at Crosshair's joke, turned and trotted home, wet and tired but without a care in the world. The car owner would be late for work on Monday. Would they care? Not them; they would have forgotten all about it by then. All they cared about was not to get caught. The time soon came for Robert to learn the pain of a bad conscience.

The shameful half-crown

After school one day, Robert was with his granny in her house in Cedar Street. He sat quietly as usual, surveying her kitchen while she worked around the room. He spotted a half-crown lying on top of the sideboard. He knew that a half-crown was a lot of money and he wondered why it was sitting there. He thought, *surely it should be in someone's purse?* As the time passed, he mused about what this money could buy. A bad thought that should not have come to him, came to him! *What if I just took it? No-one would know. It would just be as if it had disappeared. Anyway, nobody would know it was me.* This was one of those moments that occur in everyone's life, when there is a devil on one shoulder and an angel on the other.

The Devil wheedled in his ear, *"You're quite right, Robert. Just take it. No-one will know!"*

The angel murmured quietly, *"Robert. Don't be mean. Your granny or your Auntie Katie worked hard for that money. Leave it alone and be a good boy."*

The Devil, having more persuasive tones, put a soothing whisper in his other ear. *"But it's only a half-crown. They'll get another one. They probably don't even know it's there.*

*They'll never even know it's gone. GO ON! Just pick it up
and it's in your pocket!"*

The problem was that his granny was there, and he saw no
opportunity to pilfer the coin. She could turn round at any
moment and catch him in the act. He was in the throes of
wrestling with his conscience when a real voice shattered
his thoughts.

His granny spoke. "I'm just away out to the toilet, Robert.
Be a good boy till I get back."

"Okay, Granny."

When she had gone out to the stairhead toilet, he was in a
very bad state of mind. He knew if his granny had not gone
out, he would not have been in a position to pinch the
money. In that case, he would not have had to make a
decision. He now had no alternative but to make a decision.
He had to listen to his conscience and decide to be good or
bad. This confusion was causing a buzzing in his head. He
knew it was wrong to steal, but was it really stealing? He
knew it was stealing, but if it was just money that had been
forgotten then it wasn't really 'stealing', it was 'finding',
and if you 'find' something then it's okay just to keep it.
With that logic, the decision was finally made.

Moving from his chair, he went up to the big sideboard and
looked hard at the object of his desire. He feared his granny
would be back soon. The throbbing in his temple was like a
beating drum. He could hear the blood rushing in his ears.
He lifted his hand. In a flash, the money was in his trouser
pocket. He scampered back to his seat. He realised at once

that now he was a thief for stealing from his providers. He had bitten the hand of those who fed him! He had not been able to obey his 'good' conscience. He was bad and would never be the same again. The Devil had won, and he had sold his soul for two shillings and sixpence!

He was about to return the coin to the top of the sideboard when he heard his Granny Campbell coming back into the lobby. It was too late! He had no time now to put it back. He waited for another chance. Redemption never came.

He went home via the toyshop in Braco Street, and stood by the window gazing at the toys. He entered the shop and bought a clockwork mouse and some sweets and a bottle of fizzy juice. He ate the sweets and drank the juice. Before he got home to Raglan Street, he had thrown the clockwork mouse away in disgust and fury at his meanness. His conscience had switched over to 'good' mode, and he resolved never to steal again because it caused such a bad feeling inside of him and he did not want that again.

The realisation of his wickedness was already hurting sorely. His thoughts were jumbled. *It might be better if ah had been caught. Then ah would have been punished. Maybe ah should tell ma mammy? She forgave me for stealing the dinner money. That's different, though. Stealing frae Granny Campbell is horrible; ah'll get killed for that.* He was so ashamed and afraid, he was unable to confess his heinous crime. Further ideas about the theft still buzzed around in his head. *Perhaps ma Auntie Katie left it there for Granny to buy the meat for the Sunday dinner for ma cousin Michael and me? Maybe the money was for ma mammy to help her through the week.*

He would never know whether or not the half-crown was missed. It might have been there for no reason at all and no-one was any the wiser, but that is unlikely since a half-crown was a significant amount of money. The most likely explanation is that the crime was discovered and, by deduction, it was agreed that Robert had taken it. The family probably, out of sympathy for Jeanie, allowed it to be quietly forgotten. That nobody ever mentioned it to him made it harder to shed his shame for what he had done. It was a sore lesson. He resolved once more that he would never steal again. But did he?

Easy come; easy go!

Adults react to sudden riches in a variety of ways. Wealth by *inheriting* usually involves sadness and loving care in assessing the manner in which it may be spent rather than just to fritter it all away. On *winning* a large sum of money, the adult reaction involves no sorrow at all, but neither is there any guilt. When an adult finds a small sum of money, it usually ends up in their pocket, but a large sum would normally be handed into the police station.

That way came satisfaction and a possible reward for honesty. When you're only nine, life doesn't work like that. The mind of Robert operated on a simpler principle: if you find money lying on the street…it's yours. The person who lost it was careless. They deserve not to get it back. Tough luck!

He was playing in Braco Street with his pals at around half-past-three one day. It was already dark and spitting with rain. He stood looking at a piece of wet paper stuck to the ground at his feet. What attracted his attention was its shape

– a rectangle that looked like a one pound note. He bent and picked it up thinking, *this canny be a real one. Is it just a picture?* He shouted to his pals, "Hey! Look whit ah've found! Ah think ah've fun' a pound note!"

Bertie, Ian and John Carly came over to inspect his find. Gathered like iron filings round a magnet they stared in disbelief at this treasure marvelling at his luck in finding this huge sum of money. Bertie was first to comment,

"It *is* a pound note, Roburt."

"Haufers!" said Ian.

"Fuck off! Ah fun' it!"

"Ye canny hauf it between us, Roburt," said Carly.

"How no'?" complained Ian.

"Because there's four o' us, ya daftie!"

"Well, ah jist meant share it oot between us."

"Aye, but ye didnae say that, did ye?"

At this point, Robert had had enough of their argy-bargee. "Ye can aw stop fighting over ma money. Ah fun' it, so ah'll decide whit tae dae wae it, awright?"

He could have been thinking, ah'll *go into the sweet shop and ask Mrs Wilson if the owner can be found. If she says no, then the pound will be mine.* Or maybe he thought, *ah'll take it home to ma mammy and let her decide what tae dae.* It's even possible that he considered, *maybe some poor old lady dropped it on her way to buy her week's shopping, or it was a man coming home from work, sorting out his cash to give to the rent man and didn't notice it falling from his pocket.*

But he was not thinking those things. None of these noble ideas had entered Robert's mind. He had instantly decided what he wanted to do with his new wealth. "Come on! We'll spend it in the toy shop."

They ran to the shop to stare into the brightly-lit window at toys they normally could not afford. They went in and ordered four water pistols. One of the boys was sent into Mary Began's shop with the rest of the cash. He bought five Will's Woodbine cigarettes, saying they were for his daddy, a box of matches, two packets of Bengal matches, and a bottle of lemonade. The lemonade didn't last very long between four thirsty cowboys. They filled their pistols at the well at Baird's Brae. The bottle was refilled with water for extra ammunition. It was now about half-past-four, dark and wet. The sensible decision was made. They should all go to the Kelvingrove Art Gallery. There they could smoke their fags without fear of being caught by any of their family.

By five o'clock, they arrived at the great front doors of the museum and were told that the place was closing and they were not getting in. Sad though this news was, they were not too unhappy. They wouldn't in any case be allowed to smoke in the museum or play with their Bengal matches. The front of the building was shelter from the rain and a place to continue to play with their water pistols. They lit their fags. It took a while to smoke one each. They had no notion how to do this, except by sucking in and blowing out the smoke in the manner of their elders. Inevitably they got to the choking and coughing stage, which led them to conclude that smoking was 'a mug's game'. The fags were chucked away in favour of a battle with their new, super squirting water pistols. The water made little difference to them, as they were already rain-soaked.

The boys had fun frittering away their wealth. When they ran out of water, they turned for home. On the way back to Raglan Street, they disposed of the last evidence of their good fortune – their water pistols. They even tossed away the lemonade bottle that was worth thruppence on its return to the shop. Thus, there was nothing tangible to show for the money that had fallen Robert's way, except for a single box of matches. Some folk can multiply their gifts and others just waste them. On the journey home, a thought emerged from somewhere in Robert's mind. What if he had kept the money instead of wasting it? But the thought didn't last long. This was no entrepreneur. This was a young financial hedonist! He was a seeker of fun without responsibility. Round the Cowcaddens streets, this kind of *fun and games* was there in abundance to be enjoyed without guilt. There were days, though, that were quite the opposite.

Prisoner

Robert's sister Jean was rarely a heroine in his house. She was forever being criticised by her mother for fighting with Hetty and for being lazy. She never wanted to do any housework or run messages, or even just to get up out of bed at the weekend. When Jean went out, everyone heaved a sigh of relief. The third world war was not going to start today, at least not before she returned, which was hopefully a lot later in the day. The rivalry in the house was only between her and Hetty. There was no animosity shown by Jean to the two boys. The canny boys, however, on hearing the first rumblings of discord between the two girls, made themselves scarce. Rarely one got trapped in these exchanges, but they escaped more often than not. Robert was grateful, however, for one of those rare times when Jean showed her kindness.

His mother had confined him to the house for being more than usually bad. It was a beautiful summer day and the kids of the street were out playing games. Robert was stuck in the bedroom after tea. All he could do was to lean out of the window and look at the goings-on in the street below. He watched wistfully as his pals played football. Girls were doing the usual skipping rope work, while others played peever. The evening light was that lovely soft glow of summer under a blue cloudless sky. Some kids, chatting like fishwives, lay or sat on the warm concrete street. There was no traffic on Raglan Street; there was no wind. It was quiet, save for the sounds of the children, their voices ringing sharp and clear to his ears three storeys up. He knelt on a cushion by the window, constantly changing his position to relieve his sore knees.

One of his pals shouted up at him, "Hey, Roburt, c'mon doon an' play!"

"Ah canny. Ah'm kept in!"

Several times he went through to ask his mother if he could go out to play, only to meet with her blunt refusal. His misery increased with every rejection as the hours went by. The evening light began to fade. The evening sky was changing from blue to gold. The street began to clear. Robert realised that this day was gone. His forlorn wish to go out to play was unrequited. He drew away from the window and closed it gently. Picking up his cushion, he placed it back on the chair by the fireplace and sat down. His heart was sore with the pain of being punished by being imprisoned on such a perfect summer's day.

In his wretched misery, he wept quietly. The noises from the street dwindled away to silence. The shadows lengthened. The room grew dark. He snuggled into his chair. As his dejection reached its lowest ebb, blessed sleep assuaged his wretchedness. He stirred as he became aware of a gentle hand nudging him into wakefulness.

"Robert," whispered Jean. "Robert, wake up, son."

He yawned and stretched in his chair. Turning, he saw Jean and her friend, Annie McCready, both looking at him with sympathetic faces. Jean lifted him off the chair and led him to the bed recess.

"I'll get you a wee drink, son. Put on your pyjamas, and jump into bed."

Jean came back with a biscuit and a cup of milk. He sat up in bed and finished them off while listening to Annie and Jean giving him sympathy for being so sorely punished.

"But Mammy was right. Ah've been awful bad."

"Aye. So you have. But you've been punished, and it's all over now. When you wake up tomorrow, it will all be in the past. So you just go to sleep and have sweet dreams, OK?"

"OK. Thanks, Jean. Thanks, Annie."

He smiled for the first time in hours, and gave his sister a hug. Annie was smiling at him. He felt that she, too, should be hugged, and stretched his arms to her. She took the signal and gave him a hug. He almost cried again. He was not used to all this affection. Both seventeen-year-old girls smelled of talcum powder and scent. His head spun a little from this close encounter. He was in love with them.

He lay down. They tucked in his bed covers, made them up to his chin, and each bent forward to kiss him on the forehead. Jean stroked his hair.

"Oh my! You will break a few hearts when you grow up, Robert Chessar. Goodnight, son."

"Goodnight, Jean," he whispered. "Goodnight, Annie."

He went to sleep thinking all was right now with his world and tomorrow would be a better day. He was partly correct.

Lizzie's got a bundle

The people of Jeanie's family were relatively poor in financial terms but rich in aptitude for finding ways to make it through the week. One ploy involved a person taking a sheet or blanket and going round knocking the doors of wealthy houses to beg for any stuff they didn't want. This was known as 'hawking' for a 'bundle'. Robert's Auntie Lizzie had been doing this for years and making a shilling or two. One day Jeanie told Robert that Lizzie had a bundle. They should get over to his granny's house right away to get the best pick. Naturally, the items were for sale but, since the death of Jeannie's man in the war, Lizzie had given her a good discount. The bundle lay open on the floor of the kitchen and all the stuff was in a heap to be lifted and admired for size and style. Robert's mother picked up a small tartan kilt. She pulled Robert over and began to wrap him in it.

"Here, son, let me see what you look like in a kilt."

"Look at the wee kiltie!" giggled his Granny Campbell.

Robert was stunned! He wriggled free and pleaded, "Naw, Mammy. No' a kilt! They'll aw laugh it me! A canny walk in the street wae a kilt on! Please, Mammy, don't buy me a kilt!"

"Oh, my. You're no' wanting a kilt, son?" said his mother in a soft mocking tone.

"Naw!" repeated Robert, "They'll call me kiltie cauld bum!"

The women all burst into fits of giggles and quickly reassured the bashful boy that he need have no fear of that. No-one was going to put him in a kilt. Jeanie made him a promise there and then, "Listen, son, if you don't feel right in a kilt, I'll never again ask you to wear one."

Robert's fear was based on direct experience of watching a friend called Walter turning up for the annual school photograph. His mother had made *him* wear a kilt. He also had on a silk shirt with shiny pearl buttons. It was a fine photograph of the class, but may not have satisfied Walter's mother's desire to have the smartest boy in it. The teacher and the photographer both decided that the boy would be too conspicuous in front with a kilt on. Walter was, therefore, placed in the back row of the group, where his kilt was barely seen. The poor soul spent the whole day at school wearing this totally incongruous outfit. In the playground and in the classroom, his life was an absolute misery. The boys, and more especially, the girls ribbed him mercilessly.

In Lizzie's bundle, however, was a suit resembling that of a wartime aircraft pilot. It was an all-over one-piece jacket and trousers made from a dark-brown corduroy material. It was lined with wool and had a zipper from the fly to the neck for complete closure and instant warmth. Robert willingly tried it on. It fitted perfectly. He was delighted with its side and breast pockets. Jeanie bought it and he wore it home to Raglan Street.

He wore that outfit for well over a year. When he went to have the school photograph taken, his mother made sure he wore it. He appeared in the school photograph. He was in the back row – just three along from Walter. You could just see Walter's kilt, but nobody could see Robert's all-over flying suit.

Rumours

On a Friday at school, the boys were talking in the playground about a competition that was on in Glasgow. Robert was in conference with a bunch of boys, listening intently to Ian Jardine giving the fantastic details. He was animated with enthusiasm.

"The prize is a thousand pounds!"

"What for?" asked Billy Woads.

"Ye have tae collect the numbers aff motors, Billy!"

"How dae we dae that then?" asked John Carly.

"It's dead easy. Ye get a sheet o' paper, stand at the road, and write down the numbers aff the cars that go by. When you get a thousand, you send them in and you get a thousand pounds."

"Where dae we send the numbers intae?" Bertie Crosier's queried.

As if it was so obvious it need not be explained, Ian said, "Tae the Glesga Corporation Transport Department!"

"Where will we start, Ian?" asked Robert.

"Well, ah think the busiest place is St George's Road. If we sit at the pub on the corner just round frae North Woodside Road, we'll see hunners o' motors."

They were convinced. There would be so many cars there that they would have their quota in no time. All they needed now were paper and pencils, easily borrowed from school desks

After school, they settled down on the pavement at the chosen venue – the pub on the corner. They waited and duly noted the number of each car that went past. This continued for about an hour. Each had a sheet full of numbers. Five of them now had a hundred numbers to show for their efforts. A discussion took place.

"Ah've got twenty-five. How many have youse got?"

"Ah've got twenty-two."

"Och! Ah've only got nineteen."

"Youse are rubbish! Ah've got thirty-three!"

"How come you've got that many? Ah've got every motor that's went by."

"Oh, sorry! Ah took lorries as well. Who said it was only motors?"

Ian Jardine settled the rising dispute. "Listen! Motor means anything wae four wheels. That included lorries but not motorbikes or tramcars, OK?"

All agreed, and were pleased that in less than half an hour they had got so many numbers. At this rate, the thousand pounds was very soon to be in their pockets. The car-spotting continued for another hour, and before breaking up to go for their tea, they tallied up their score. They had nearly three hundred.

The next day, being Saturday, had the gang assembled early for a concerted and final attempt to achieve their target. If they could get a good couple of hours in, then they would be on the way to being incredibly wealthy. All they needed was a couple of hundred numbers each and their dreams were realised.

"Are we still collectin' lorries or jist motors, Ian?" asked Robert.

"Ah think it's still motors and lorries, Roburt. Bit we're gettin' loads o' motors. Lorries probably arnae needed anyway, OK?"

It was hot. This was the summer time. They were thirsty. Robert ran round to Missus McCready's door and swallowed a huge cup of cold water with the usual thanks as he dashed away back to his post. Others had defected to their own watering places and returned with undiluted enthusiasm for car numbers. That is, until the hot sun put an irresistible temptation in their way.

The heat from the sun had some effect on the stone pavements, but the tramlines on St George's Road became very hot. The metal rails got so hot it was not possible to touch them. In between the rails and the granite causey stones, the tar started to melt and expand. It seeped out in shiny spheres, jet-black and glistening in the sunshine; irresistible to small boys. Using pencils and sticks, the boys collected these globules of tar for use as quasi-marbles. The small projectiles were secreted in their trouser pockets.

By mid-afternoon they compared notes and were pleased to realise that their undertaking was at an end. Each of them had more than two hundred numbers carefully noted down on their grubby, tar-stained notepapers.

Ian was pleased to report to his troops, "That's well over a thousand, so we're aw gonny be rich!"

He gathered in the sheets to make a complete document ready to take into the offices of the mighty 'Glasgow Corporation Transport Department'. There was a quiet interruption from Bertie Crosshair, "Hold on a minute. Should it no be different numbers we send in? They numbers arnae aw' different!"

"Aw shite!" exclaimed Ian. "We should aw have sat at different corners! We've really only got two hunner numbers!"

No-one spoke. Presumably, like the rest, Robert was mentally reviewing their poor planning. He stood, looking at the pavement thinking, *ma share would've been two hundred pounds. Ah could've bought a bike each for John and me. There would've been plenty left tae buy a fur coat for ma mammy.* The stunned team realised their awful stupidity. It had dawned on them too late what an adult would have guessed in seconds. Robert was sure that they were all feeling the same desperate sense of disappointment that he was experiencing. All that money! Gone! No sudden riches were to be theirs!

Ian Jordan looked really unhappy as he turned away mumbling, "Ah'm away hame!"

The rest of them acted out the same dejected exits from their field of dreams. It was a disappointing day for all of them. Robert had more to face when he got home. It wasn't so much that his black trousers were dirty from sitting on the pavements. It was worse and much more embarrassing. The white linen trouser pocket was stuck with melted tar onto his leg.

The remedy was, in one way, rather painful. His trousers had to be pulled off like an Elastoplast – hard and quickly, which made him yell. The other part of the cure was very embarrassing. He had to stand still in the sink, wearing only his underpants while his sisters rubbed the affected thigh with margarine to soften the tar. Before long he was the possessor of one pure-white leg and one dark-brown leg. Soap and water restored his normality except for his face, which was scarlet till he got trousers on again. Hetty and Jean were no strangers to this long and frenzied process of tar removal from his legs.

"How many times have you two done that for him?" asked Jeanie.

"I've lost count," said Hetty.

"That tar gives a lovely tan to his leg, though. Doesn't it, Mammy?"

"Yes, Jean. You two should use it when you're going tae the dancing."

"Oh no! We would smell like tarry boilers and rancid margarine!"

They all had a good laugh at Jeanie's not-too-serious suggestion. Nothing could replace the application of calamine lotion and an eyebrow pencil line down the back of the leg to simulate nylon stockings. Robert, cleaned and ready for his tea, advised his mother and sisters how his day had gone from bad to worse. The sticky tar was bad enough, but his failure to become rich was very frustrating. He explained the efforts to which he and his pals had gone to in order to make their fortunes. He was not amused at their incredulous laughter.

"Well. Ah was gonny buy a bike each for John and me, and a nice fur coat for ma mammy. Ah'm not being funny, so you can stop your laughing!"

Jeanie squeezed the nape of his neck with affection as she whispered in his ear, "That will teach you not to listen rumours, Robert. There's no such competition going on at all. Someone's been pulling your leg."

"Aw no!" he wailed. "Aw that time wasted fur nothing!"

Robert's days did not always end in such *desolation*. Some were topped by *elation*.

Sad old man

The children in Raglan Street grew fit in any number of ways, without actually being aware. The hard work they did was mainly involved in having fun. A frugal but adequate diet ensured that *most* of the kids were not fat, or at least not grossly overweight. The environment they lived and played in was perhaps the biggest contributor to their overall fitness. It offered so many energetic activities. Some had special significance for Robert. Situated in Lilac Place, a cul-de-sac just off Garscube Road, there were five air-raid shelters. These had flat roofs of reinforced concrete. Built close together, they were about thirty feet long by ten feet wide and eight feet high. The gaps between them varied from a few feet to about eight. It was possible to jump from one roof to the other. This group of shelters was called the 'Lilac leaps'. This was a favourite spot for adventurous kids on warm sunny days and evenings.

The kids played 'tig', skipping ropes, peever and, of course, long-jumping over the gaps. As is the nature of kids, there was lots of noise, shouting, and shrieks. Most people enjoy the sounds of children having fun, but there was always an exception. One man in particular was always complaining at the kids to be quiet and go away. He lived 'low down' in a house in St George's Road. His backcourt adjoined Lilac Place but was separated by a high brick wall and washhouse.

The boys and girls from Raglan Street sometimes ran through his close as a short cut to the 'Leaps', as they called them for short. They had to climb the backcourt wall onto the midden roof and, from there, jump onto the nearest air-raid shelter. This old man objected to the noises in his close, in his backcourt, and coming from the high-level adventure playground of the kids. Some of the youngsters took a detour round Garscube Road to Lilac Place to avoid his bad temper and the walking stick he wielded.

Robert and his pals grew tired of this man's intemperate vituperation. Most of the kids were of the same frame of mind and just let the old guy rant for a while until he got fed up and went back inside his house. Strangely enough, there was no time any of these kids gave cheek back to the old man. It seemed that there was a sense of respect for his age and instinctive understanding that he had a point, so they tried to accommodate him. When he was in full voice, issuing his commands, they stopped their games and just stood still, looking at him like robots till he stopped. They had learned this method over time, passed from the older ones to the younger kids. He was unnerved by this odd behaviour.

The short instruction handed down the years was, "Jist staun' still an' look it him. Don't say anything. He canny touch us up here."

When the old man finally felt rather foolish at shouting louder than the people he was trying to quell, he turned and went back into his close. When they heard his door bang shut, the children resumed their games, making less noise as requested. But this did not last long. Then the old man would reappear, waving his stick and shouting up at them, only to receive the same silent attention (and respect?) till he had again run out of things to bawl. One day, when he was in full voice for the umpteenth time, a window higher up was flung open.

A woman's head popped out and she fired a salvo at the poor old guy. "Hey, you! You're making mair noise than these weans. Leave them alone! Away back intae your house and gie us all peace!"

He looked up at her, shrugged his shoulders, turned and went away. The noisy jumping games resumed. Robert grew fitter and stronger. The high-level leaping gave him the feeling of almost being able to fly. Running fast was stimulating, but being up high on the air-raid shelters was exhilarating. He mused, *Ah want tae dae something bigger than this.*

Jump!

The first flight of stairs up to Robert's house at 27 Raglan Street had thirteen steps. The second flight up was only six steps. Robert's desire to fly often found him jumping down the six steps in one leap. All other flights to the top were ten steps, but these were too much for a wee boy to jump, so when he got to the six, he jumped with confidence and made as much noise in landing as he could to increase the drama of his brave action.

Charlie Brown lived on the first landing. Robert called him *Chick*. They met one day just as Robert had launched himself down his flight of six.

"Well done, Robert. Why not jump down the bottom stairs?"

"Aw, Chick, that's a bit high for me tae jump. Ah hivnae tried that before."

What was Chick thinking about by asking him to try such a daunting thing?

"It'll be all right, Robert. Ah'll stand at the bottom and catch you."

He took a position at the bottom of the stairs and signalled the boy to go ahead and jump. Robert was looking at the flight path he would have to take to get airborne and arrive at the bottom without hitting any of the stairs. This meant he would have to jump high…but then he would hit the underside of the of stairs above. He would thus bounce off the ceiling, fall onto the stairs, and then roll down in a heap and suffer great pain or die.

While the boy pondered the difficulty of choosing his best trajectory, Chick grew impatient.

"Come on! Robert, jump! Don't worry, I'll catch you. It's just like flying"

The reference to flying threw a switch in Robert's brain. He began revving up his engine to reach the proper speed of take-off. He placed one foot at the edge of the stairs, leant back on the other foot some distance behind, and began to sway his body and arms backwards and forwards to gain the optimum launch angle.

Once again Chick shouted, "Come on, Robert! I'll catch you."

He assured Chick that he was about to jump, but was not quite ready yet as he did not want to hit the roof. Sometimes in life there occurs a delicate and timely juxtaposition of two things that are so mutually interdependent that a planned action works out perfectly. In the case of Robert and Chick, the necessary coincidence of actions required Chick being at the bottom of the stairs when Robert arrived by air. With this thought, or something like it in his mind, Robert made the decision to launch himself fearlessly into the chosen trajectory, hoping to arrive at his destination and be safe in the strong hands of his reliable friend.

Unfortunately, the same thought had just left Chick's brain. He simply felt that his challenge to the youngster was too much for the wee boy. He decided at that moment to leave and went into the back close. He never saw Robert jump. He heard him yell, though!

"Chi-i-ick!"

Then he heard the thump as Robert hit the bottom of the stairs and rolled out into the close mouth. Knowing now that his challenge had been accepted, Chick ran back to see what damage he had caused.

The boy was lying face-up on the ground. He was grinning!

"Robert! Are you okay, son? Can you stand up?"

"Ah'm awright, Chick. Did you see me jump they thirteen stairs?"

"No, son, but I heard you. I'm sorry. I went away. I thought you wirnae gonny jump!"

Robert got up and brushed the dust off his trousers. He assured Chick it was okay. He was just a bit bruised and sore, but his smile showed he was pleased with himself. Chick was puzzled how he had made this crazy jump and ended up in one piece, smiling like a Cheshire cat.

"Robert, how did you land without hurting yourself?"

"Och, it was easy, Chick. Ma big cousin Bertie taught me how tae land. He's a paratrooper."

"Oh well. I suppose that explains it then."

"Chick!"

"What, son?"

"Ah jumped aw they stairs and ah didnae *need* you!"

"You did well…but promise me you'll not do it again?"

"Naw! Ah've done it once, that's enough!"

Chick walked away shaking his head. Robert stood looking up the flight of stairs thinking, did *ah actually dae that?* He turned and walked out of his close. He was smiling.

"Ah FLEW!"

EIGHT
1952

Up till now, Robert's lifestyle had not changed very much. Neither had he noticed any major changes in his family's lives. Hetty, Jean, and his mammy all worked, and his big brother was at the senior school. Apart from the odd domestic altercation, everything seemed to be going along just fine for him. He was ten years old, as yet innocent of those more adult attentions that were about to affect his sense of happy wellbeing; stimuli that would very soon alter the way he regarded other people, his pals, his family, and himself.

He had sweet memories of his 'Uncle Frank' but saw no signs of his having a replacement. Jeanie still indulged her love of dancing, but since Frank went away, she never brought another man home. On the other hand, Hetty was going steady with her fiancé and planned to get married in June. In order to do that, she was receiving instructions from a local priest in order to convert from Church of Scotland Presbyterianism to Roman Catholicism. Jean seemed to have settled down a bit, and held a good paying job as a typist. She had a steady boyfriend from Cedar Street, where Granny Campbell lived, so it was felt that he should be okay. So far, she had shown no signs of settling down and getting married.

John spoke to Jeanie about leaving school early instead of staying on for his 'Highers'. He wanted to get a job and start earning real money. Jeanie was disappointed but she agreed. There were only two provisos. John should get a good trade. A tradesman earned twice as much as a labourer, and the prospects of promotion were much better. Secondly, she stressed he was never ever to think of joining the army.

Robert was still at primary school. Although he had just turned ten, he was becoming aware of aspects of life that he would never think of discussing with anyone in his house. He was growing up. Other people were beginning to notice; not all of them were as benevolent as his big pal Chick. He was also to learn valuable lessons about the risks of life. Jeanie had got him to help her a bit more with the chores of the house, one of which tested his initiative and altered his attitude to others who took risks on his behalf.

Wee Spiderman

Robert was first home after school. John had a long walk from his school. The rest returned later from work. This meant he could start getting things done to prepare for their evening meal: setting the table; peeling a few potatoes; or any other useful tasks to help his mother. It worked well until one day he got home to find that he was locked out. The key had not been left in the normal hiding place. He sat down on the stair trying to figure out a way into the house. His conclusion was that it was not possible. The house was like a fortress, all locked up with no way in bar the big, solid, bolted front door. But he had an idea. A plan formed.

He went down to the backcourt to find a small boy. His idea was simple: bring the littlest fellow upstairs, lift him up, and push him through the small high-level window into the inside toilet. The window was always open. There were two vertical iron bars fixed into the stonework. The gap looked wide enough to allow a small boy to get through. Once inside, he could nip round and open the front door from the inside.

Two suitably-sized helpers volunteered. They trooped up the stairs behind him to consider the problem first-hand. One of them said he was too big, turned round, and left. The other agreed to have a go. He stood on Robert's shoulders, grabbed the iron bars, squirmed like a monkey, and got his legs and torso through. Another twist and his arms were through, his hands tightly gripping the bars with only his head sticking out. The little fellow was now out of Robert's reach.

"Roburt, ah'm stuck. Ma head willnae go through."

"Ye huv tae get it through! Ah canny reach up! Try again!"

"Roburt! Ma arms are getting sore."

"Oh Jesus! Stay there! Ah'll try tae get you down. Don't let go or you'll choke tae death!"

The small cat burglar was so taken by this suggestion of his impending death that he began to howl for his mother. This fearful display of raw emotion had Robert at a complete loss. He was jumping up and down, wasting energy, in a vain effort to reach his little choking burglar, whom he was about to be responsible for killing between the bars of his inside lavvy window. He stopped his dancing, stood still, pressed hard with this hands on his head, trying to squeeze out a method of saving the wailing waif.

Above the bawling, he heard a familiar noise. It sounded rather like his house door being opened from the inside! Fearing that he was hearing things and this was just his mind hallucinating for a means to free his victim, he ignored the sound.

Then he heard a small voice, "There's your door open, Robert."

In a flash, Robert was standing on the toilet seat, lifting the half-strangled boy by his bum to get him back out the way he had tried to get in in.

"Get your arm and shoulders through. Hang on tae the bars. Ah'll come round tae the stair and catch ye, OK?"

"Aye, ah'm okay," gasped the wee chap, now much relieved and no longer sobbing for his mammy.

Robert brought him safely down and made him sit on the stair. Looking at the boy who had opened the door, he said with gratuitous disbelief, "Ah canny believe you just did that. How did you get intae ma hoose?"

"Och! A jist climbed up the drainpipe and got in through the kitchen windae."

"What! You must be daft, ya wee monkey. Ye could have been killed!"

Before Robert could say any more, the gallus wee boy blanched, turned round, and shot down the stairs, obviously afraid he was going to get in trouble for such foolhardiness. Robert stared after him for a few seconds thinking, *Jesus! Ah could've had two dead weans. One splattered in the backcourt and the other hung on the lavvy windae.*

He put an arm round the other wee boy. "Don't you run away, right? Ah'm gonny bring ye something frae the hoose."

He came back and gave the lad a couple of pennies from the gas meter money that Jeanie kept in a jar on the mantelpiece. The kid trotted away down the stairs shouting his thanks.

Robert did not tell Jeanie. *Least said, soonest mended,* he decided. There was no way he was going to tell her about nearly strangling a wee boy or the incredible stupidity of the unknown wee Spiderman climbing up the thirty-foot-high drainpipe.

Robert never did find out who he was. He had simply gone. An uninvited thought invaded Robert's brain, *A loose bracket on the drainpipe and he would have been gone... permanently, and me not able tae save the other frae choking! I would have been put in jail for killing they two wee weans!* He shuddered.

Danny the tough guy

Some of the older boys in the street had very violent natures. Some others were not always as hard as they liked to think. Robert's cousin, Big Danny, for instance, had some rather strange ideas of how to conduct himself in civilised company. When he was at their Granny Campbell's house, he was always the perfect gentleman, saying all the right things in as pleasant a manner as his brain could muster and with an angelic smile of innocence on his face. The smile was out of place on a visage that had seen the end of many fists. It would not be wrong to suggest that he looked like a boxer who always came second. Out on the street, however, at the age of fifteen, he acted the 'hard man', spewing Anglo-Saxon expletives to confirm it.

This was a boy who could cry when holding a new baby in his arms and ten minutes later would be kicking the daylights out of some youngster in the backcourt. For Robert to be in his company was scary, so John was careful to avoid Danny being alone with his youngster. He saw to it that Danny was kept away. John was a tough fighter, but steered clear of street-gangs. He had fought and thrashed Danny when he was younger, and had a psychological advantage over him. If John said *jump*, Danny jumped.

It happened that a bunch of boys were playing in Big Danny's close at the bottom of the street. John was there, but had taken his eye off his wee brother. Robert was leaning against the wall, waiting to see what the big boys were planning to do next. Danny came over, stood in front of him and then moved closer. He was starting to press Robert to the wall with his stomach. Robert looked up. He stared into Danny's emerald-green eyes, framed by his weird smiling face. The youngster was not afraid; he was trying to guess why Danny had an odd, far-away look of happiness. Some instinct told him that Danny was not completely in charge of his actions.

Although Robert was only ten, he was alert to the strangeness of this behaviour. This was not the kind of thing a big boy should do with a wee boy. His big cousin should be protecting him. Here was Danny doing the opposite. Danny was threatening him in some way that he was not yet sure of. He was unclear, too, of the reason for this strange bodily contact that he had never had before. The close was full of other boys. He thought, *surely they'll see this and stop it?*

Danny took Robert's hands in his and stretched them above the boy's head so he was pinioned against the wall, quite unable to get free. While wriggling to get away he mumbled, "What are ye daen', Danny?"

Danny whispered with a gravelly voice, "Ahm showin' you what boys dae tae lassies, Robert!"

Still holding the boy's hands up high, Danny started to slide down lower so that his face was level with Robert's. He smelt Danny's bad breath and saw the saliva in his mouth.

"Ye haud them like this so they canny get away, and then ye kiss them!"

Robert was *now* very frightened. He could not imagine that his big ugly cousin was about to kiss him. He turned his head to the side to avoid the smell and the contact. If he were to be kissed, it would have to be on the ear! The whole episode lasted a few seconds. Robert had gone from puzzlement to terror in that short time. It was time to end it. At the top of his voice he bawled, "Danny! Don't dae that!"

Robert heard another loud command from the side of Danny.

"Get aff ma youngster, ya bastard!" John screamed.

The next second, Danny was violently shoved to the side. John was on him like a cat. The two of them fell onto the hard floor of the close. Danny grunted at the impact of the cold stone on his shoulders. John had noticed what this big fool was doing. He was old enough, unlike his wee brother, to understand the borderline that Danny was about to cross. In a rage at Danny's trespassing on his kid brother, John punched him hard on the left ear with his right hand and on his nose with the left. As he sat astride the now sobbing body of his cousin, he yelled, "Danny! Ya fucking pervert! Dae that again, and ah'll kill you!"

"Ah wisnae daen anything, John. Honest," bawled Danny.

"Look, you! Ah saw ye! Touch him again and you're deid! Get it?"

Big hard man Danny slunk off through the back close. John took Robert away home and warned him again never to be alone with Danny.

"Danny's dangerous, Robert. He might try tae hurt ye again."

"How would he want tae dae that, John?" asked the boy.

"Robert, remember when Mammy warned you aboot Joak Dan?"

"Aye."

"Well, that time it was Joak *Danny*. Keep away frae him. Right, kid?"

"Okay, John. How did he want tae kiss me?"

"You're too young for me tae tell you. It's what Joak Dan does tae wee boys like you. It's no' nice, so stay well clear o' people like him. Okay?"

"Aye."

Robert had learned something that day, but he was not very sure what it was. It wouldn't be long till he began to understand. Thankfully, sometimes there was no lesson to learn; just innocent fun to be had and to enjoy.

Tyres to Milngavie

Give a boy a wheel and a stick, and he will roll it along the ground. He will run along beside it all day long. There may be a fine psychological reason for this phenomenon. In cultures around the world, boys will roll wheels or tyres around the streets, the obvious reason shows on their faces – pure fun. Raglan Street was no different. One sunny Saturday morning. Robert, his brother John, some cousins and other boys were running around with tyres from cars, motorcycles, and even a lorry. Someone had a gird-and-clique; a circle of iron propelled by a hand-held loop of steel fixed to it. It was just after lunchtime when someone suggested they all go on an expedition.

"Where tae?"

"The West End Park?"

"Naw, the parkies'll chase us oot."

"The 'stinky ocean' then?"

"Naw, it's mucky there. We'd lose the tyres in aw that mud and muck."

"Ah've been tae Mulguy. We could go there and play in the river. There's a wee beach o' pebbles doon at the laundry and it's shallow. Ye can paddle in the water."

This got unanimous approval. They set off right away so they could have some fun before coming back for tea. Word had got round and more drivers joined, making the posse up to twelve strong. The party set off down North Woodside Road, rolling their assortment of wheels and tyres. Robert had a lightweight tyre from a motorcycle, and his brother had a car tyre. One boy had a tyre off a bus. It was very cumbersome to push and to steer properly. He was a giant of a lad, so he was managing quite well on Maryhill Road heading uphill to Queen's Cross. The pavements were busy with shoppers and others. Some seemed to enjoy the sight of the boys having fun. Others just moaned as the kids skilfully guided their tyres past them, going in single-file until they were out of the busy parts.

From the Maryhill police station, they had another steep climb from the under the canal bridge up to Fingall Street. Then a level run past more shops parallel to the canal. Beyond the tram depot, the long straight road alongside Dawsholm Park was deserted all the way to Canniesburn Toll. That was a good place for a rest and to make sure the younger ones negotiated this complicated junction safely.

So far no-one had dropped out, except for the giant with his heavy tyre. He couldn't push it any more, so he left it to be retrieved on the way back, and helped out with the youngsters.

On they went, keeping well together, through Canniesburn, Hillfoot, Roman Road 'y' junction, and Kilmardinny. They halted at Alexander's bus garage to stare in wonder at a strange railway structure standing about thirty feet off the ground that ran on stilts for about three hundred yards. Slung on a monorail underneath was a cigar-shaped rocket.

"What's that thing?"

"Don't know."

"Dae ye think it's a rocket tae go tae the moon?"

"Naw! A rocket tae the moon would go up the way, no along the way."

"Oh?"

"Aye. We'll see it some other time when it's finished. Then we'll know what it's fur. Let's get moving."

They rolled on quickly to reach the tram terminus at Milngavie Cross. On up the hill and down the other side they found the laundry. Here was the River Allander wending slowly through the shallows over a wide shingle bed. Beside that was an inviting expanse of grass where they could all lie down and rest. Journey's end; except they had to go back.

They had completed a trek of six miles and were elated to have found such a beautiful place to rest and to play for as long as they wished. Shoes and socks were discarded, trousers rolled up and into the water they went to splash and be happy. Some doffed their trousers and had a swim, some if not all of them had a drink of the cold and clear water. No-one cared that they had brought nothing but themselves and their tyres. This day out would cost nothing except effort.

Hours later, the group was mustered and counted. They set off on the return trip. One detour was taken. They went down Garscube Road from Queen's Cross. This was an easier run into the top of Raglan Street; they got home quicker but nobody really cared about the time. No-one was lost or injured. It was a very successful and enjoyable round trip of twelve miles. They all agreed that they would do it again. They did, but not with tyres; it only cost a penny return on the tram. That was another kind of adventure, but Robert yearned that maybe someday he could go to Milngavie another way – on his very own bike; one of a few unfulfilled dreams. Dreams come true, but sometimes there's a cost.

Cheerio Mr Singh

"Hey, Roburt! See if you won the pools, whit would ye buy?"

"Ah'd buy ma mammy a new hoose, a fur coat, and ah'd buy a blue Vindec."

"Aye. Me tae. Come on roon tae Ram Singh's for a look at the bikes."

Robert and his pals all wanted bicycles but hadn't the money to buy any. Whenever they had scraped a few shillings together, kids in Raglan Street hired bikes from shops. When Robert loitered in the hire shop, he experienced something sensual from the mixed aromas of rubber solution, oil, and paint. He wanted a bicycle so much that he saved any parts he found. Given time, he would satisfy his obsessive longing and one day would build one of his own. His yearning was so strong that he hung around the hire shop, even when he had no money, just to look at them and smell the odour of place. He just wanted to be around wheels and pedals. It really upset him the way the owners of the shop carelessly stacked them against each other. *The owners don't care enough for their machines. If ah had one o' them, ah would keep it in the house. Ah'd oil it, keep the tyres pumped up, fix the brakes tae be really tight, and ah'd get a dynamo for going out at night. It would be a cracker! Everybody would be that jealous o' me. Ah would cycle aw day and never have tae take it back tae the shop.*

Ram Singh, an old Indian man, ran a cycle repair shop in St George's Road. Ram's small shop was open long after the hire shops had closed. He could be seen at night through his brightly-lit shop window, surrounded by untidy shelves crammed with new and second-hand spare parts. This Aladdin's cave fascinated the local bike-less urchins. They idled in the shop, talking to the old man, watching him work. He was a bit scary to look at. His skin was shiny, like oiled leather. A thick gold ring through the side of his nose looked sore. Another bigger ring in his ear held a green gemstone. His mouth had a constant grin, showing his yellow, crooked teeth. The smile was more of a smirk, but since Ram Singh was an ugly man anyway, the kids figured the look on the old guy's face was not out of place.

The smell in the shop was the same as the hire shops, with an added pungent curry odour from the old man's breath. Robert and his pals liked to watch him working. They listened intently as Ram explained why there were ball-bearings; how to break a chain and insert a new link; how to tighten the cones without stopping the wheels from turning; why pedals had left and right-hand threads; how to adjust a saddle…and much more. This was a valuable education for Ram's un-bonded but willing apprentices.

The old man took a liking to Robert, seemingly because of his eager and innocent interest in learning. What else could it have been? Ram, in his low and mysterious voice, answered all the boy's questions, putting his face close to Robert's and engaging the boy's eyes with his own. Robert was so intent on his tutor's lecture one evening, that he hadn't noticed they were alone. His pals had drifted away.

Ram invited him into his back shop to show him how to repair a puncture.

"You pump up the inside tube and hold it under the vatter in the sink. Ven you see the bubbles, you know vere the puncture is. See the bubbles?"

"Aye, Ram. That's clever."

Ram then showed how the tube was dried and scuffed before the rubber solution was applied.

"Now ve have to leave it for five minutes before the patch is put on and sprinkled vit the chalk. Ve have to vait for about ten minutes before the tube can be pumped up again, so I vill put a new tube in to save time, OK?"

"OK, Mr Singh."

"Vould you like to have a bicycle of your own, Robert?"

"Oh aye, ah would love that Mr Singh, but ma mammy canny afford tae get me one."

"Aw, too bad! Maybe if you got a job you could get a shiny new bike, eh?"

"That'll no be tae ah grow up."

"Maybe you can have one now? You could come here and vork for me, eh?"

This sudden offer caught the boy's attention. Here was a golden opportunity he had not thought of, but he was unsure how it would work. He decided to find out.

"How could ah work fur you?"

Ram Singh showed that pleasant smile you see when someone has just caught a little fish. He issued his invitation, "Come here and hold this veel for me."

Robert moved over to where Ram was putting the new tube and tyre on the wheel.

"Hold the veel with your hands on the spokes, there and there, Robert."

"Like this, Mr Singh?"

Ram's voice became softer as he answered the boy, "Yes, Robert. Hold it tight. Tell me, have you got a girlfriend?"

"Naw, ah'm only ten. Boys at ten don't have girlfriends, Mr Singh."

Ram moved a little closer to the boy. He whispered another question to his young protégé.

"Vell then, do you have a boyfriend, Robert?"

Robert flicked his head round to look at Ram, as if to confirm that he had actually asked that odd question. Ram was looking at Robert with his old, penetrating eyes. His eyebrows were raised in expectations of an answer. His gnarled face had the trace of the usual grin. This time it was not as friendly.

The boy looked down at his small fingers tightening on the spokes of the wheel. He had gained a moment to think about the creepy signals from the old man's face. He decided that Ram was not aware of the queer meaning of his last question, and mentally forgave him. He turned and answered with a nervous, boyish giggle, "Naw, Mr Singh. Ah've got boys who're ma friends but ah don't call them 'boyfriends'."

He hoped that this would satisfy the old man's curiosity. But he was wrong. Ram moved his face closer to the boy, and with a look of menacing mockery, he asked another question that seemed to Robert more like a demand.

"Vell, Robert, would you like to be *my* boyfriend?"

At this unwelcome suggestion, Robert winced. His mind was suddenly alert. His brain cancelled his previous pardoning of the old man. Ram had finished the tube insertion and was leading his helper over to the bicycle to refit the wheel. His hand was on Robert's shoulder. He told him to fit the wheel into the front fork and apply the nuts. As Robert was doing so, Ram brought his hand to a lower position on the boy's back. The hairs on the nape of the child's neck started to tingle.

He felt that Ram Singh was not being friendly. He wasn't sure why he felt like this. There was a voice inside his head saying, '*Be careful*! *Is this another Joak Dan?*' He flicked his eyes to the side, furtively measuring the distance to the open doorway. He knew he should give an answer but was wary in case the old man made any sudden move on him. He decided to say nothing to see what Ram would do next. He braced himself to be ready to run.

Noticing the boy's reluctance to answer, Ram tried another gambit. Stroking the boy's fair hair, he spoke in a gravelly voice, lower now than before. "You are a very good vorker, Robert. You should come to my shop after school and vork for me. In no time you vill have a bike of your very own. Vat do you say, eh?"

Robert noticed, with each passing word, Ram moved his hand lower. It was pressing below the line of his snake belt. He could feel the heat of the old man's hand through the thin cloth on the backside of his trousers. The boy's face reddened with indignation and embarrassment. His heartbeat was loud enough for him to hear it.

Easing himself away, he turned his back to the door and faced his former friend. Ram Singh had become a danger. The old Indian had crossed a forbidden line with the youngster. His brain was racing, searching for a clever reply, *Ah didnae like whit he jist did, and ah don't like how he keeps offering me things. Ah'm no scared o' him, but ah jist don't like him!*

He felt bold enough to give an answer. "Thanks for offerin' me a job, Mr Singh, but ah think ah'll wait tae ah grow up."

"But I have made you a good offer, Robert. Vat is wrong?"

Watching the old fellow feigning surprised hurt, Robert smiled. He was still blushing with anger and annoyance but was conscious of a growing feeling of bravado. He was in charge of himself as he spoke quietly.

"Ma mammy widnae let me work for you, Mr Singh. Ah'm gonny wait tae she buys me a bike, so ah'll no need one frae you."

The old man's smile returned. It was not a nice smile. It was a smile of distaste. It was the smile of someone telling you he did not like you for what you had just said. He said nothing, but Robert got the message from his look. The boy now felt guilty that he had misjudged the attentions he had received. He had not really intended to hurt Ram Singh. He had some knowledge of the intimate goings-on with people. Kids in Raglan Street knew what men and women did and how a baby was made, but this affair with his old mentor was new to him. It puzzled him. Maybe Ram was just being friendly.

But the old Indian was still giving the same look of disdain. This unchanging stare of contempt for the boy was the turning point for Robert. He decided that he was not to blame. It was Ram Singh who was wrong. He would not blame himself. He remembered how uncomfortable he was when the old man caressed his body. He made up his mind. He did not care to have Ram as his friend and teacher any more. The best way was just to leave his shop.

"Cheerio, Mr Singh."

The youngster turned and walked through to the front of the shop and into the street. Outside, he stopped. Gazing through the window, he took a final look at the old man. Ram was standing in the back of the shop. Their eyes met. The boy sighed and turned away. This was the man he had trusted and respected, but he knew he had made the right decision.

As he walked home, he had bitter thoughts. *That's me lost ma chance tae get a new bike. It'll be a long time before ma mammy buys me one.* Although he felt he had learned lessons, he was again not exactly sure what they were. One thing was clear, though, he was proud of his action. But inside he was angry; angry at losing the chance to work and earn a bike. It was Ram Singh who had offered that chance. It was also Ram Singh who made it impossible to accept that offer.

He didn't hate the old man. Not hate. That was too strong. He was not annoyed, because that was not strong enough. The innocence had certainly gone from his association with Ram Singh and his beautiful bike shop. In this confused and unhappy state, Robert walked slowly along St George's Road, through Braco Street to Raglan Street, where he met his big brother at the mouth of their close.

"Hi Robert. Where've you been?"

"Round at Ram Singh's, John."

"Who were ye wae?"

"It was just me and Ram."

"Just yourself? Were you no' scared?

It would have been easy for Robert to say what had happened. His instinct was to say nothing. The youngster was afraid to talk about it. For one thing, he might get blamed for what happened. For another, John might go crazy like he did with Big Danny, and go round to the old man.

He gave his brother the simplest answer he could think of. "How could ah be scared, John? Ram Singh's a nice auld man."

"OK, Robert. Fancy a race up the stair?"

Robert was in front all the way till the top landing where, as usual, John held him back by the pants to again finish in a dead heat. It was easy for Robert to admire his brother and some other grown-ups he knew, but there was another man who fell on the wrong side of his admiration, like Ram Singh, but for a different reason.

Mr Allen

Mr Allen was a bad teacher. He belted children for getting sums wrong. He belted them for being late. He was known to forbid a pupil from going to the toilet. "You should have gone before you came into the class!"

There was no joy in the man. None of the children liked him. They very quickly identified teachers as 'friend' or 'foe'. It was wise to stay out of Mr Allen's way anywhere inside the school, especially in the boys' playground. This bully was on duty one day after dinnertime when the school bell was rung early. Most of the pupils were not even back in the lower playground. When they arrived, he commanded them, "All of you stand against the back wall!"

On the pavement above, a group of parents watched through the railings as this scene developed. After a while, when he was sure there were no others to come, he went over to the line of boys, slid his belt from where it was hidden on his shoulder under his jacket and spoke. "Right! Who's first?"

He began to belt each of the thirty-odd children. By the time the sadistic Mr Allen had belted a few, the horrified parents were showing their indignation.

"You stop that, you bloody bully!" screamed one woman. "Don't you dare belt any mair o' these weans, or ah'll get the polis tae you!"

The rest joined in to shout similar threats. Totally ignoring their pleas and threats, Mr Allen continued his onslaught on the hapless kids. Mr Kerr, the headmaster, arrived on the scene, anxious to find out what all the noise was about. He was aware that the bell had gone early and was astonished to see his colleague belting the boys, especially in full view of some parents.

He shouted at Mr Allen, "Why are you assaulting these children, Mr Allen?"

"They are late for school, headmaster."

"They are not late. The bell was early. Give me your strap! You have no right to belt them, and you have no right to shame them by doing so in public. Go to my office. I will talk to you shortly!"

Looking up to the railing mothers, the headmaster apologised and promised them, "I am so sorry you had to see this disgraceful display of bullying by my colleague. I assure you I will deal with this most severely and he will never again belt a child in my school. Thank you all for making it possible for me to stop it with your loud and proper warnings."

To the pupils who had been belted, the headmaster said, "I am sorry you seem to have been given the tawse unjustly and in public. I am pleased you took it, in spite of Mr Allen being wrong. He will not escape *my* punishment, boys. I have taken away his belt so you will never have this problem from him again."

The boys accepted his diplomacy and his promise of swift justice for the misguided Mr Allen. The high-level audience of parents applauded and cheered as he entered the school to carry out his pledge. Mr Allen was made to go round every class to apologise for his actions. His belt was taken and kept in the headmaster's room. He was told to send any wrongdoers to the head's office and never again to punish them by himself. Robert was amongst those belted that day, but happy with the headmaster's words. This was a man he could respect. Mr Allen left the school shortly after, never to be seen again. Not all stories of the tawse were so easily dealt with. Not all teachers who belted these boys were disliked. Not all of the schoolboys had such a keen a sense of justice as Robert.

Mr Sergeant

Robert had another unusual experience with a teacher's belt. This time, it was from an old and loved teacher. There is more to getting belted than just physical pain. Honour, justice, and respect also play their parts. This favourite teacher was Mr Sergeant; quite the opposite of the cruel Mr Allen. He was the image of the famous actor, Wilfred Hyde White. His face was gentle. His nose and cheeks were covered with very thin red veins. He was a most pleasant teacher and a bit of a comic. This was the man whose joke Robert had relayed to his mother, "If at first you don't succeed…suck sausages!"

Mister Sergeant entered the class one day and slightly misjudged a fracas that had developed in his absence. He called some boys, including Robert, out to the front and was administering the 'tawse' once on the hand to each of them. The belt from this gentle man was not very sore, but nonetheless it was an ignominy in front of one's peers.

When it came to Robert, he refused to hold out his hand because he had not been part of the guilty group. Twice he had been unjustly belted: Mr Allen the most recent; and when Marshall Cower told lies about him some time back.

"Hold out your hand, Robert," said his good teacher.

"No!" was all he got back, in Robert's most polite voice.

"But you must take the tawse, Robert," said the old man.

"Ah don't have tae take it. Ah've no done anything wrong."

Robert was at a loss as to how to describe the injustice of this situation. He was hoping that his respected old teacher would understand. Robert would never want to embarrass him, but this had to work both ways. This punishment went against Robert's sense of fairness and justice.

"Well, Robert, you just go and stand in the corridor. I will see you shortly."

The old man was perhaps hoping that the privacy and the loneliness of the corridor would encourage the boy to accept his punishment and his teacher's verdict. This tactic did not work. The boy was sent to the office of Mister Kerr, the headmaster; the final arbiter. The threat of the headmaster would surely bring the matter to a close?

Robert went where he was bid and stood outside the door of the headmaster's room. He did not fear Mister Kerr, because he was a fair man and would not let this happen. Mr Sergeant arrived to continue his appeal just outside the head's door.

His efforts were in vain. Unsure of his next move, he told Robert to return to the corridor outside the classroom. He appeared some time later to ask the boy once again to accept his punishment, and once again the offer was refused. So he said, "Well, you will have to go down to the headmaster's office again. I will see you later."

As far as Robert was concerned, this little pantomime was going on too long. On the way to the appointed place, he had clear thoughts. *Why am ah in a place where people want to punish me for nothing? Why should ah walk up and down these stairs aw day? Ah should be in ma class enjoying the teacher's company and jokes. Ah'm no taking the belt just to please Mr Sergeant.* It was the logic of a ten-year-old. He would absent himself from the school and never go there again. Ever! So he left the building, climbed over the gates, and went up to play in Raglan Street.

His cousin, Jean Mathieson, found him on his own in mid-morning, playing at the foot of the street. He was happily sitting on the kerb splashing in a puddle when he heard Jean's shocked voice. "Robert Chessar! Why are you not in school?"

"Ah ran away."

He was immediately taken up to his Auntie Maggie's house and given some milk and a piece and jam. When Robert's mother came home, it was already after school hours, and she decided that Jean Mathieson should take the boy back the next day. She would explain his behaviour to the headmaster, along with a plea for leniency. That night Robert told John what had happened. His big brother was sympathetic, but gave his sage advice to his youngster,

"Robert, Mr Sergeant is a good auld teacher. You canny make him look silly in front o' his class. When you go in the morra, take the belt."

"But, John, it's no fair, Ah wisnae daen anything."

"Listen! That disane matter now. Mr Sergeant knows that. Promise me you'll jist take the belt and that's it aw done. OK? He'll think you're a wee hero and he'll no hurt ye."

Next day, Robert found himself in the class with his favourite teacher.

"Robert, please come out to the front."

The class was silent as Robert went to the teacher's desk. He stood with his back to the class looking up at his tutor. The rest of the class had seen the drama of yesterday and were obviously very keen to see the final outcome between the two antagonists. Would he take the belt, or would Mr Sergeant be forced to send him down to the headmaster once again?

The silence was broken by a soft voice. "Robert, I am going to ask you to hold out your hand. Will you do that, please?"

There was no promise of leniency here, but there was something in the way Mr Sergeant spoke that gave Robert an inkling that the teacher was in a difficult position. His big brother was right, he couldnae make his teacher look silly. It was not in Robert's nature to further embarrass his kind master. He had already done enough of that by refusing his punishment in front of the class, and by running away as well. In the same way that he had felt an injustice the previous day, he now understood that the teacher had to be seen to be in charge, and the only reasonable action was to hold out his hand. He made his first adult decision.

"Yes, Mr Sergeant."

Robert held out his hand and expected that his teacher would give him one hard belt with the strap...but he was wrong! This wise old man, with his bumbling demeanour, took his strap, with his right hand holding one end, and with his left hand held it in a perpendicular position. He then released the top end of it such that it fell gently through ninety degrees onto Robert's palm. He felt the leather tickle his hand and that was his punishment.

The class applauded the scene, glad that the drama had ended amicably for both Robert and their kind teacher. Robert looked up at Mr Sergeant and said quietly, "Thank you."

Mr Sergeant bent down and whispered softly to his discerning pupil, "No, Robert. Thank *you*."

Candles for the Wash House

St Joseph's Church down North Woodside Road was a favourite place for children who played around the streets. It was always open and it was warm. Robert and his pals, although being of the Church of Scotland, had easy access to this building. Roman Catholic churches held great appeal; this one was a fascinating art gallery. The priest watched wisely whenever Robert wandered round with a couple of pals. They were agog at the statues of the holy figures showing the 'stations of the cross' with the gory details of the suffering of this man Jesus. Although the boys were impressed with their surroundings, they had come on this visit with the express intention of leaving with some candles.

The hovering priest witnessed these seemingly innocent incursions. In acting to appear as good little Catholics, the kids lit candles and set them up on the candelabra. After carefully crossing themselves in the Catholic manner, they slowly rose and left by the nearest exit. During the process, more candles were secreted in their jerseys than were lit in the church. These stolen ones were for lighting their gang hut at night.

There was never a time when the priest 'saw' any candles being 'liberated' from the church. The urchins prided themselves that they were cleverly fooling the old man. Time and again they raided the candle boxes, and time and again they got away with it. Surely they had to be excellent 'knockers' to do that so often without getting caught? Robert thought, *as long as the church was very wealthy, it would not miss a few candles.* Perhaps the same thought process was in the mind of the good Father of St Joseph's Roman Catholic Church. If so, God bless his benevolent soul! He was not to know the real purpose for which these items were purloined.

"Where're you gaun, Roburt?" asked his big brother.

"Doon tae the chapel."

"We don't go tae the chapel, ya daftie! We're Prodissants!"

"Ah know, John. Ah'm jist gonny knock some candles."

"Oh! That's okay then. Jist don't get caught, right?"

The youngster sped off on his mission. He had to hurry, as it was getting dark. The candles were to light the hideout – the washhouse in the backcourt. Robert had had an invitation from an older lad, John Arran. "Knock some candles for the washhouse and you can be in our gang."

One of the others had protested, "He's too young! He's only aboot nine, for fuck's sake!"

But John Allan was the boss. "He's goat tae learn sometime and it might as well be the night, so you shut it!"

Robert was glad of this chance to be in the gang, but puzzled about what he was supposed to be learning. He was thinking, *Ah'm an expert at stealing candles. John Allan should know that. Maybe it's something else they're gonny teach me the night?*

In no time, he was back with six candles – his passport to the inner sanctum. The virgin candles were lit and secured to ledges round the walls. The place was cold, but it was warmer the closer you got to the roaring fire below the boiler. The privileged ones perched on the warm metal lid of the boiler. The soldiers hunkered down in the two big clay sinks, while the recruits stood around the walls or sat down on the cold concrete. Not quite sure where he was meant to be, Robert stood in the middle of the floor. He had no idea what to expect, but he was soon to find out when the banter began.

"Ah was out wae Jessie Corrigan the other night. She let me touch her tits."

"Naw she didnae! You're a liar. You've never touched a lassie!"

"Ah have so touched her. She even played wae ma willie. She's good at that."

"Did she go the whole way?"

"Naw! Ah wanted tae but she widnae. She took *me* the hale way though. Ah think ah'm gonny marry her."

"You're aff your heid, Carbide! You don't merry a lassie jist because she gives you a wank."

"Hey, youse two! Jessie's ma cousin, so stop talking aboot her like she's a whore!"

So continued the claims, accusations, and counter-claims. This unfamiliar and lurid language fascinated Robert. He knew most of these words, but seldom heard them in such numbers while he was present. *Maybe this is what ah've to learn?* he thought. The youngster didn't understand all of what was being said, but he was no angel. His own encounters with lasses had only been clandestine kisses, but he knew already that the thing he peed with had other uses of a more delectable nature.

His musings were disturbed by the sudden darkness as the candles were blown out. In the dim firelight he became aware that his newfound friends were preparing to enjoy the fruits of their own appendages. The dim firelight provided discretion, but ensuing odd noises, giggles, and sighs made Robert uneasy. He looked this way and that in the gloomy room. *Whit are they aw daen? You arnae supposed tae dae that in a gang!* He almost started to laugh at the funny noises and gyrations of these supposedly tough guys. *They aw look stupid!* Although he was not afraid, he was a little mystified that something so private should be shared so openly. *If this is what's needed to be in their gang, then ah'm away!*

The noises grew in pitch and tone, turning from giggling to more breathless sounds. The door of the washhouse opened quietly and closed again. In the dimness, the other boys were too far gone to notice Robert's defection out into the darkness of the backcourt. This lesson in the dark did not compare with the one he got in broad daylight.

Holy wine on the church roof

From the kitchen window of Robert's house could be seen the gable end of the derelict church in Lion Street. An annex to the church had a pitched roof, one side of which made a valley between it and the gable. This was a play area for the boys and girls of Raglan Street. It was skilful to stand with your back against the church, push off the wall, and run up the pitched roof of the annexe and back down again. There was no real danger, but if you slipped on the slates, you rolled ignominiously back down into the valley to land at the feet of your jeering pals.

It was here that Robert and a half dozen other boys got a new, open-air demonstration of baby-making equipment. An older boy was telling them all about a certain action on the body produced a white wine, and it was this that made babies when it was put into a girl. Nothing but clear proof would persuade his audience who were incredulous but eager to learn the mystery. The challenge by his doubting disbelievers could not be resisted.

He was forced into providing a demonstration. "Stand round me in a circle so naebody can see me frae thae windies."

He leant his back against the church wall, undid his trouser buttons and, to the amazement of the rest, demonstrated very clearly the art of self-stimulation. There were gasps not only for the demonstration that was taking place, but also for the size of the implement being used. Inevitably, the boy shivered and shouted that they should look. They *were* looking. They were *impressed*. He was right about the wine! He recovered his privacy and proceeded to explain how the wine should find its way into a girl. Scepticism returned to the gang. They drifted off. Robert, however, was intrigued by the final part of that lesson. Given the chance, he felt it might be fun to give it a try.

Behind The Empress

Most people never forget their first experience of the joys of life. Ask anyone and they will tell you what it was like. Ask a man and he will lie about it, especially if he was a late developer. No man wants to say it happened at the ripe old age of twenty-five. He will say he was in his early teens, and it was fantastic. The definition of first encounter is taken as complete loss of virginity, but surely the loss of innocence qualifies as well. If it does, then it happened to Robert when he was ten!

One warm summer night, when the kids in the street were flocking together looking for some mischief, it was agreed they should troupe down to the lane behind *The Empress Theatre* at St George's Cross. Latterly it was called *The Metropole* and was owned by Glasgow's comedian and impresario, Jimmy Logan.

There was a show on every night. During the performance, the group of youngsters arrived at the rear of the place. It was very dark apart from the faint glow from a waxing moon, giving each of the boys and girls a pale ghostly appearance. Some older ones started to kiss each other. This was a popular example of how to pass the time, and most of the rest followed suit. Only the very youngest, like Robert, were unsure of what was expected of them, but were willing to try this new pastime.

Robert was standing at one of the theatre's exit doors set back into the building about four feet. In the shadow of this, he was pursuing contact with an older girl from the street by giving her a kiss on the face. She at first appeared shy, like him, and was not co-operating fully in the new game. From across the lane could be heard the squeals and giggles from the more experienced and active couples. Suddenly his companion said to him that she wanted to show him a certain secret area of her anatomy. When he queried which that part was, she pushed him back a little way and, with a deft movement, she was showing him her bare midriff and below in the darkness.

"Ah canny see anything," he said.

"Feel it!" she said, taking his hand and guiding it to her favoured spot.

247

"Feel whit?" he asked, puzzled at this development. "There's nothing there."

"That's where you put yours," she whispered, and slowly put her hand where he was not expecting.

She was leading him to a place he had not been to before. He was not sure how to continue this journey, but he was quite certain that he needed to. He asked what she wanted him to do. She suggested that he should set free the little prong now attempting to escape from its prison in his trousers. Always an obliging boy, Robert agreed, and in a moment he was proudly displaying his eagerness for her to see. As she pulled him close to her body, he let out a yelp of delight as their tickly bits touched. She giggled with a similar sound of pleasure, and was keenly wriggling to get more from the new experience, when suddenly the lights above the doors flickered and lit up. The patrons of the theatre were about to surge from the building.

This sudden change in the seclusion and privacy of the rendezvous caused very fast reactions. In a trice, there were speedy recoveries of decorum and a disorderly mass exodus from the lane, amid sounds of glee and groans of disappointment. This experience of the two youngsters could be described as a complete loss of innocence and, by implication, could be construed to represent a loss of virginity. It may be, however, that the author is stretching a point. Whatever it was, Robert learned another valuable lesson that night, and this time he had no doubt what it was! The lesson on the church roof was now completely understood! He was nearly eleven, but was as yet nowhere near to making a baby.

New Year Customs (Green Ginger Wine, etc.)

At the end of each year there were no big rowdy parties in Robert's house. Jeanie felt it was disrespectful to the memory of her husband for her to make merry so near to the date of his death. For good hospitality, she always had something to offer any family or friends who came by to wish her the season's greetings. John and Robert were duly instructed to go round to the licensed grocer's shop and bring back two special purchases.

The first was a bottle of Crabbies green ginger wine. This was what their mother allowed the boys to drink. She would not allow them to partake of any alcoholic beverages and was very strict in her observation of this rule. She was the one to pour out little measures for each of the boys when the time came to usher in the New Year. What she didn't realise (and the boys did not let her into the secret) was that this nice little drink was not free of alcohol but was in fact fairly well laced with the stuff! It said so on the label, but Jeanie never saw that. It had been strategically torn at that small spot.

The second item was a bottle of sherry. Not just any old sherry! Oh no! It had to be *South African Table Bay* sherry. No-one knows why she had a fixation about this particular brand, but she would not have any other, and that was that! The boys didn't mind at all that they were not allowed to drink this. They were quite content to get slowly and happily stoned on Crabbies green ginger wine!

When the strokes of midnight were chiming and all were standing to celebrate, Jeanie observed a custom that had been handed down to her by her parents. She went to the window, opened it wide, and said goodbye to the Old Year. She then opened the front door to welcome the New Year into the house. This was something their family witnessed every year, and it was quite moving to see the sincerity with which Jeanie carried out the ceremony and the respect shown to her feelings as she did so. She was also dedicated to the idea that everyone should be in their own house at this time of the year unless for some reason they were not able. In that case, they should at least be in the home of a good friend.

A period of chatting and some singing followed the arrival of the New Year. Soon after midnight came the noisy departure of the guests, and bed for Robert and the family. Jeanie was permitted the luxury of a long lie in bed the next morning. Now that Hetty was married to her beau Allan Shannon, young Jean was free to indulge in the same privilege of a long lie in the bedroom. Robert and his brother, fresh from their sound 'drunken' sleep, rose early to set about cleaning the place up.

First thing was to drain the glasses of Table Bay, Crabbies, and any beer that had been left the night before. The kettle was put on to boil for washing up the plates, glasses, and tumblers. The fire was set and lit to welcome their mother and sister into the world again. Cigarette stubs were lit and smoked for mischief, but chucked in the fire along with those in the piled-up ashtrays. The house was quiet and secure. There was no noise at all outside. The soft sound of snores from their sleeping mammy, cocooned in her bed, was a dividend that the boys didn't get very often; she was always away so early to her work.

They woke her with a cup of tea and put a match to her cigarette to be enjoyed in bed before she turned over to continue her luxurious lie-in. This little ceremony was a pleasure for the boys, to give something back to their hard-working, long-suffering mammy.

NINE
1953

The New Year brought some welcome changes in the house and the family. Since Hetty's wedding in June last year, Robert had more space in bed. Jean was, for a while, in the big bed with Jeanie. He and John had the bed recess. Hetty had moved into her new husband's home, where his brother and sister, both unmarried, still lived. They had three bedrooms, dining room, kitchen, and a bathroom. That proved very convenient for the newlyweds; Hetty very soon got pregnant and was expecting her baby in June.

Jean, in the meantime, had not been careful with her boyfriend and was also expecting her own baby in May. The upshot was a hurried wedding in February when Jean became Mrs Dalziel. Jeanie decided that she would sleep in the fold-down bed settee in the kitchen, leaving the boys in the recess with the whole bedroom to themselves. John had arranged an apprenticeship and was soon to leave school at sixteen, to start his work. Robert's knowledge of life had grown in an extraordinary fashion in the last year. He had learned a lot more about human behaviour than other eleven-year-olds. He now understood that people are not always what they seem to be on the surface.

Life was complex, but he was feeling more confident about how to survive the many pitfalls of living in Raglan Street.

He would have to be careful, weigh people up more, look for danger signs, take advantage of any pleasures that present themselves, and not get caught out by deceptive friendship. This mind-set was to stand him in good stead as he continued his adventures with his three pals, Jardine, Carly, and Crosshair. He did not realise that by the end of this year he was not to see them again. The changes in his home life were relatively insignificant compared to what lay in front of him; changes beyond anything he could have dreamed possible. For the moment, though, he carried on as usual.

Razors!

It was the Easter holidays from school. Robert and his three pals were up at the canal. They had been playing for hours on the giant raft of wooden logs that had lain for years in the basin at Firhill. The 'Nollie' was a quiet place except for the far-away sound of cheering from inside the Firhill dog track, plus the noise from other kids playing round about the area. Carly was poking something in the water.

"Carly! What are you daen?"

"Ah'm trying tae reach this fitba', Robert."

"Don't stretch too far or ye'll faw in," said Ian Jardine. "Pull it back wae this stick."

"Wait the noo! It's no' a fitba', it's got a heid! Ah've found a deid dug!" shouted Carly.

Bertie Crosshair came running over for a look. "It's aw bloated up! It looks like it used tae be a greyhound. Poor bastard! Must've never ran fast enough."

They threw stones at it, trying to burst it open, but they just bounced off. Their noise had attracted some other kids who were drifting over towards them. Ian noticed them and whispered, "Ah think we've got company."

"They might be frae Hamiltonhill," said Robert. "We better move away fae them, just in case, eh?"

"Aye," said Carly, "They can turn on ye like wildcats. Ma mammy says, *he that turns and runs away, lives tae fight another day*."

"We're no' *gonny* fight wae anybody," said Robert.

Firhill was not quite a 'no-mans-land' for these Cowcaddens boys, but they could not be certain that the local boys were friendly. It had been a sunny summer's afternoon when they came to Firhill. There were grown-ups walking about the place, giving the boys a feeling of safety. Now, hours later, the four youngsters had not noticed that the adults had drifted away. They were the only ones left as they sidled away from the local crowd. Although the early evening was still bright and warm, the place began to feel very large and empty.

Carly spoke quietly. "Ah think it's time we wirnae here. Ah want tae get hame. Are youse coming?"

They turned and walked slightly faster than usual back along the canal bank. Some distance from them was a fence across the pathway. They had to negotiate that on their way home. Two people were there. One was sitting on the gate and the other leaning against it.

"Who are they, Bertie?" said Robert.

"They arnae men. They've got on long trousers but they're still no men."

"They arnae wee boys either," said Carly. "Somewhere in-between, ah think."

There was something about them that didn't look right. Robert had that same tingly feeling on the back of his neck when something isn't quite the way it should be. He slowed to an easy walk. He guessed by the way that his pals had also slowed down that they were having the same sensation. They seemed also to know that stopping dead in their tracks would give the impression they were scared. They did the natural thing that street-wise kids do. They walked slowly with their hands deep in their pockets, to give the impression that they were not in the least bit bothered by the two teenagers. John Carly began to whistle. Robert was thinking, *that might help?*

As they continued their approach, Robert's heart was beating so hard he could hear it. His plan was to get to the fence, casually climb over it as if nothing was wrong, then walk away to safety. The fellow leaning on the gate had other ideas. He stood up. They all stopped. He asked a simple question.

"Dae youse boys want tae get by us?"

It was more of a challenge than a polite request. Robert replied, trying to sound casual, "Aye. We're on the way hame."

"Wait the noo! Ma pal's gonny show youse some tricks wae a razor."

Bertie Crosshair answered in a squeaky voice, "Naw. It's OK. We just want tae go hame."

Robert felt like he was going to pee his trousers. He was really scared at the mention of a razor! The gangs where he lived used them in fights. His cousin had been cut across the face with one. They were terrible weapons. With his mouth agape, he stared at the boy on the gate who had opened his mouth and stuck out his tongue. Flat on it, lay a double-edged Gillette razor blade!

"Look at that!" said John Carly. "He's got a razor in his mooth!"

The boy flicked it. It turned over and went between his two front teeth. Next thing, he took his fingers and pulled the razor blade straight out from between his teeth.

Robert screwed up his face in horror at the thought of the blade cutting through the boy's gums. *These two nutcases are up tae something. Ah thought they were only playing aboot, trying tae impress us by blocking the gate, then he produces a razor! This is definitely impressing me anyway! Ah feel as if ah'm being hypnotised. Ah'm too close tae them tae run away...they'd just catch me. We're trapped! Ah canny take ma eyes aff the razor.*

Not content that he had transfixed the wee boys with his first trick, the gate boy pulled another one. He held the blade with his thumb and forefinger with a sharp edge on each lip and closed his mouth. Robert began to panic. *This dope must have escaped fae the loony bin. If he disnae stop playing wae that razor, he'll cut his lips and gums tae ribbons.*

He instinctively shouted, "Watch whit you're daen! You'll cut yersel'!"

His warning had no effect except for the chilling warning from the razor magician. "Ah'm no gonny cut masel. Ah'm gonny cut your throat! You're gaun intae the Nollie!"

Bertie Crosshair started to bubble. Ian Jardine shut his eyes trying to make it all go away. Carly sat on the ground with his face in his hands, moaning softly. Robert froze. This was it. He was going to die. His mind started to assess what his chances were. *There's naebody here tae help us. Ah can hear the crowd in the dug track cheering like mad. How can they cheer when me and aw ma pals are aboot tae get done up? Probably gonny get killed wae this daft murderer. It disnae seem right; that crowd's happy when we're scared tae death. We'll end up aw swelled up like that deid dug in the watter. Weans'll be chuckin' stanes at us! Ma poor mammy; she'll have tae stand looking at ma stinking body, blown up like a balloon.*

Robert felt the razor boy's eyes boring into his, leering at him the way you see a bad man in the pictures, face all screwed up, smiling that evil smile that says, *ah'm gonny dae something really bad tae you, son.*

"Whit's your name, you?"

Robert swallowed hard. In school, his teachers were always saying, *tell the truth and shame the Devil!* This time he thought it was better to tell a *lie*. A *big* lie! Instead of saying he was Robert Chessar, he said, "Ah'm Francis Foy, fae Lion Street, doon in the Coocaddens!"

The guy jerked up and fell off the gate. "Wait the now! Are you Joe Foy's wee boy? Joe Foy, the Glesga razor slasher?"

"Aye! Ah um! So youse two better get off yer marks, 'cos any minute now he's gonny be up here looking for me and ma pals!"

The two half-daft hoodlums jumped over the gate and took off, stumbling like three-legged greyhounds – funnily enough, going the same way as Robert and his chums. Now the tables were turned. The wee boys from Raglan Street were scaring the daylight out of the two ne'er-do-wells. Robert felt good. That was the day he started to feel what it's like to be powerful! Not with razors...just words.

Hunger

Boys are always hungry. No matter what good fare is provided in school or at home, if boys are presented with an open opportunity to eat well, they will never refuse. The boys in Grove Street School were no exceptions to this characteristic condition.

Opposite the headmaster's house on Grove Street was a tenement with a pend. This was a feature of many of these buildings, to allow a horse and cart to gain access to a factory or workshop built in the backcourts. In this case, the factory was used for making a hard biscuit-like foodstuff.

The product was loaded into hessian bags for transport to various customers.

During the school lunch hour, the boys toured the surrounding streets as an extension of their playing area. One place to go was through this pend into a large backcourt with good dikes to climb and play on. To get there, they had to pass the side door of the factory. There were always bags of the product lying open outside. Perhaps they were discards from the production line that had got broken, or had not met with the high quality standards of the makers. Often they were warm, having been recently baked.

Predecessors of Robert and his pals had sampled these. They handed down the news that these things were not only edible, but were quite good to the taste. They were like lightly browned scones, tasting of flour mixed with salt and fat. They broke easily for sharing out. Altogether they were not a bad addition to the daily diet of the scavengers. Many a snack was had from this free food source. There was no danger of being penalised because no-one ever came to say they should not take the stuff.

There were times when one of the workers came out with more bags. They never bothered with the kids who had obviously helped themselves and who stood around munching happily. One man was in the habit of referring to the boys as *his wee calves,* but Robert didn't understand why he should give them that name. He learned that these biscuits had no ill-effects. On the contrary, he was convinced they were a good for you because of that. It was years before this particular 'wee calf' realised that the factory was in the business of turning corn, soybeans, sorghum, oats, barley, salt and linseed oil into…cattle cake!

Q.V.S.: *Another world*

At the end of May, Robert was in his classroom in Grove Street Primary School. It was the last period before leaving to go home for the weekend. His teacher, Mr Sergeant, had a note passed to him by another teacher. The school bell rang.

"Right, boys and girls, clear your desks. Off you go and have a good weekend. Robert Chessar, please wait behind till everyone leaves."

When the class had gone, he called the boy to his desk.

"You are to go downstairs to meet your sister, Hetty. She's waiting for you outside the headmaster's office. I remember your sister very well. She was in my class a long time ago. Please tell her Mr Sergeant was asking for her, will you?"

"Yes, Mr Sergeant."

Robert was puzzled but did as he was told. Unbeknown to him, Hetty had arranged a meeting with Mr Kerr. She took Robert by the hand, knocked on the headmaster's office door, and waited. Mr Kerr appeared and ushered them both into his room. He told the boy to sit on the chair by the window. He was not invited to take part in their discussion. It was normal for him to be seen and not heard. He listened to their small talk, but paid little attention since they seemed not to be talking about him.

"It's a while since you were in my school, Hetty. I see from your letter you are a married woman now. Mrs Shannon, I believe?"

"Yes, Mr Kerr. I was married last year, but I still take a close interest in my family's welfare. I try to help my mother as much as I can."

Hetty set about explaining the reason for her visit. Robert had lost interest in what they were saying, but by catching the odd word he realised that they were discussing someone's future. Some of the comments made him pay more attention. He became a little uneasy. It seemed that somebody's future was about to become less comfortable. He wondered, *who is it they're talking about?* Hetty was clearly making a request to Mr Kerr.

"I think it will be a great benefit for him to go there. I only need you to endorse the consent forms."

Go where? thought the boy.

"I'll do all I can to help. What is so special about the place?" asked Mr Kerr.

"Well, Queen Victoria School in Perthshire is a military boarding school for the sons of Scottish soldiers. He is a lonely boy and has difficulty making friends. I am certain the school will be the making of him."

Lonely? Canny make friends? It canny be me then.

Hetty continued to describe the benefits of the boarding school. There were sporting facilities, hundreds of boys to make friends with, and a regime of exercise, fitness, and discipline. Above all, there was also the promise of a fine education.

"It will be just perfect for my **wee brother** during his secondary school years."

Oh no! It is me. They're sending me away!

The conversation continued and Mr Kerr occasionally nodded his agreement. Robert fidgeted on his chair; trying hard not to let his emotions show. He decided to stay quiet until he found out more. The headmaster said, "That's fine, Mrs Shannon, I'll sign the forms. Do you have them with you?"

Hetty handed over some papers. The headmaster studied them for a few moments, added some written notes, and duly signed in various places before returning them to her.

"Thank you very much, Mr Kerr. Now I can send these off to the school."

"Is there a problem with his age?" asked the headmaster. "He is now eleven-and-a-half. I noticed the entry age is actually nine years."

Now I'm saved! I'm too old to go!

"No, I've checked that with the school. They make special dispensation for an older child who has lost a parent in the services. As you may know, our father was killed during the war."

"I did know that, Hetty. It's very sad, but I'm sure that all will work out fine for your young brother. Give my regards to you mother for me."

Aw! There's nae escape!

Mr Kerr wished Hetty the best of luck with the application He smiled at Robert, saying what an opportunity this would be. Robert didn't speak to Hetty during their short walk back home to Raglan Street. There was, however, a lot going on in the boy's mind. He was contented in his primary school. John had told Robert that he was soon to go on to the secondary school. That would be a big change, but his big brother would be there for a while. That feeling had been a comfort to him, but this new development was alarming. He had no idea where Perthshire was. He wouldn't have his brother or any of his three pals to go with him. He would be on his own.

He would wait for a chance to ask his mother why she was sending him away. Until then, he would discuss it with no-one else, not even Hetty. At home, he dropped his schoolbag on the floor saying, "Ah'm going out to play, Hetty." Swiftly turning round, he ran down the stairs to the street to play with his pals. They asked him why he had been kept back in the classroom. He refused to tell them. He felt ashamed at being sent away. That was not to be shared with them.

Four weeks later, he was with his mother on a bus heading to Perthshire. She was taking him to sit the school's entrance exam. About a mile past Dunblane, they stepped onto the road outside Queen Victoria School, crossed over, and walked up the long steep driveway towards the impressive school building.

In the weeks preceding this visit, Jeanie did her best to answer Robert's questions, trying to allay his fears about going away. She felt that clarity and honesty were the best ways to deal with his very obvious fear and uncertainty.

"Will the school exam be hard, Mammy?"

"I don't think it will be too bad, son. It's set for boys of nine and you are nearly twelve, so I think you'll pass it easily. That depends on whether or not you actually want to get into the school."

"Mammy, ah'm not very sure. You and Hetty say it's the best thing for me but ah'm frightened. John isnae going to be there, or any of my pals."

"You'll find it's different from your life in Raglan Street. I think you will be so busy doing lots of things there that you won't have time to be worried. I know you will make new friends."

Jeanie hoped she sounded convincing but, like him, she had similar concerns for her son's wellbeing. She tried to give a good account of the positive things she had learned about the place.

"There's over two hundred boys there and they all wear the same clothes. That way you won't feel different from them. You will be in the junior part. There will be some nine-year-olds. I think they will be more nervous than you. The rules are like the army. Disobey orders and you get punished. If you stick to the rules and do what you're told, you will get rewarded."

"How dae you know that?"

"Your father was in the Territorial Army before he went to the war. He obeyed the rules and they made him a sergeant. He could give orders to the private soldiers and he got paid more money."

"Will ah be dressed like a soldier?"

"Not all the time. Just when you are on parade. Then you will wear a kilt and an army jacket."

"Mammy! You never said ah was tae wear a kilt!"

"But, son, everyone else will be wearing a kilt. You would look silly if you were the only one NOT wearing a kilt."

He was quiet for a while as this horrendous revelation sank in. He was recalling the time when he was eight. His mother had reached into a 'bundle' of second-hand clothes at his granny's house, lifted up a kilt and held it around him. He was shocked and horrified at the thought of walking down Raglan Street with a skirt on. His pals would make his life a misery. That image in his mind gave way to another. *Ah suppose it would look a bit silly if all the boys in this new school had on their kilts and there's me only in ma breeks?*

But he was still not convinced. He would still have to come home on his own and wear a kilt in Raglan Street.

"When ah come home for the holidays, will ah have a kilt on?"

Jeanie saw immediately what he was getting at. This clever question was a clincher. Answered wrongly and Robert might refuse to go to the new school. She had to find an equally clever response, one that would not provoke his rebellion. She explained what was expected of him if he became a pupil. He would live in the school and come home during the holidays. He would wear a kilt and army jacket for church parades and whenever he was out of the school.

She went on, "That means when you are on leave for the holidays you will come home wearing your kilt. The difference is that you will be dressed like a soldier. Just like your daddy looked when he came home as a soldier. He was respected because he was wearing a uniform. The folk in Raglan Street will respect you in *your* uniform."

He mulled this over. Jeanie hoped he would see the sense of her persuasive arguments. Robert had to accept he had to abide by the rules or he would not be able to get into this school. She was concerned that he might spoil the exam paper. She had no control over what he did in the examination room. She wanted to reinforce the benefits of the school to bring the boy round. Short of commanding him to go in any event, she preferred to have him make up his own mind; as long as it was a *yes*.

"You will not be in your kilt all the time. You will be in trousers and jerseys like all the others. In a way, that is another uniform. You will have your own bed to sleep in. There's hot water to wash in and playing fields to play in.

You will learn to shoot real guns with real bullets. You will not get any of that at home."

Robert weighed these facts. *It sounds better than living in the tenements of Raglan Street. Ah would be silly if ah didnae go tae this school.* Shooting real guns sounded like an exciting prospect.

"Ah think this'll be a good place for me, Mammy."

Jeanie took that as a *yes*. But he continued to press for more information.

Their arrival at the school's imposing entrance left him open-mouthed at the size of the place. It was higher than the tenements in Glasgow and was covered in green ivy. He was unable to speak. They entered and were led into an oak-panelled central hall. On a wall hung a full-size painting of a boy in a kilt and scarlet jacket. A Glengarry and tartan plaid made him look very smart. He had fair hair. Robert was impressed. Jeanie and her boy mingled for a while with about forty other boys and their parents.

An army officer called their attention, read out the names of the boys, and led them into an adjoining classroom. The two-hour test had begun. Jeanie and the other parents were taken for tea and given a tour of the school. During the walk-round it was advised that only twenty places were available. Half of those boys in that classroom would not be joining Queen Victoria School. Jeanie said a silent prayer for her son.

The letter from the school commissioners came three weeks later. Jeanie opened it quickly and read it slowly. She sank back into the cushions of her fireside chair. She wept.

Robert had been accepted. He was to report to the school at 11am on Monday, 27th July, for induction and to take up residence. His clothes and other belongings were to be taken away by whoever accompanied him. He could keep a maximum of one pound in cash and some personal items like a toothbrush, pens, and writing materials. The school would provide everything else he would need. His ration book had to be brought and surrendered to the school bursar. Jeanie had about a week to get him ready, but there was one small problem.

Doctor Ashby

"Mammy, ah've got a sore thumb."

He showed her his finger. It was green under the swollen skin in the corner of his nail.

"Yes, son, it looks like you've got a whittle."

"Whit's a whittle, Mammy?"

"It's a poisoned bit on your finger."

"Will ah die wae the poison, Mammy?"

"No, son. Is it sore?"

"Aye. It throbs and it's a wee bit sore when ah touch it."

"Right then, we'll get you to bed. I'll take you up to see Doctor Ashby tomorrow."

Robert fondly remembered the good old doctor. He had been to see him many times in his life. When safely tucked up in his bed, he mused over warm memories of his meetings with the old family doctor, *another visit to Doctor Ashby. Ah like that. Ah've been to him a few times. Once he even came tae the house when ah was in bed wae spots. Ah was in the bed recess wae curtains drawn across so it was dark to let me sleep. When the doctor came in, he pulled back the curtain. Ah remember his deep friendly voice,* "Will you let me have a look at your spots, Robert?" *Ah liked him. He was kind. The thing he pressed on me was cold on my hot skin. Now I've to visit him the morra. He always knows my name. He always says,* "Well, Robert. How is my wee chap today?" *His soft voice always makes me feel that I could trust him. He smelled of tobacco, just like my Granda Campbell. My granda smelled o' burning paper as well, though. He always lit his pipe wae folded bits o' newspaper poked intae the coal fire. Sparks flew everywhere! Granny called him an auld josser! His tobacco gave that lovely smoke smell and then it was okay. Doctor Ashby smoked a pipe. Ah'd seen him in his surgery lighting it wae a sparking lighter that smelled ae petrol. When ah came in, he put his pipe doon in a clay ashtray on his desk. It was still burning and gein' oot that same 'Granda' smell. Ah think ah might like Doctor Ashby better than ah like my granda. My granda just sits and smokes and grumbles at my granny. But the doctor looks at me, touches me, smiles at me. In a way, he's like a daddy...especially when he smiles. That makes me feel good. It's as if he cares for me.*

He fell asleep.

Next day, Jeanie and her boy were seated together in the waiting room of the doctor's surgery in Garscube Road. They tried to get comfortable on the hard wooden benches, with their backs resting against the planks of varnished pine on the wall. The ceiling was miles above that. A long electrical wire hung down, holding a tin lampshade that looked like a Chinaman's hat. The bulb was lit but did little to brighten the room. In the gloom, Robert eyed the people as they came in and shuffled to find their places.

Aw the folk are trying no' tae look at anybody. Some look no' well. Others act like they've brung the sick ones tae see the doctor. Some o' them look no' well as well.

The miniature reception hatch slid up. A woman's head appeared. It instructed Jeanie, *please go in now, Mrs Chessar.* Jeanie tapped the door, waited for a 'come in, please', and entered. Doctor Ashby swivelled round in his chair.

"Well, Robert. How are you, my boy? You've got bigger since I last saw you."

"Ah think ah'm not well. I've got a whittle."

"My, my! How do you know that?"

"My mammy told me."

"Well, let me have a look at it, Robert." He prodded it with his finger.

"It's sore when you touch it, Doctor."

"Yes, I see. You have what's called a whitlow. Mrs Chessar, I would like to let this develop for about a week or so. It is inflamed but I would like it to come to a head so that I can release the soreness. Bring him back in a week or ten days."

With his specs teetering on the end of his nose, he looked at Robert. In his deep friendly voice, he tried to reassure him. "Now, Robert, you are going to be fine but you have to keep your sore thumb out of harm's way for a while. No playing or fighting. Just rest. When you come back, I will make it better. Do you understand?"

"Yes, Doctor, but it's really quite sore just now."

"Right, Mrs Chessar, keep him inside, preferably in bed. He must be rested and calm to avoid the poison spreading."

"Thank you, Doctor."

She took her son home. The youngster was disappointed that his worthy doctor had not taken away his pain. He thought perhaps he had not said clearly enough how painful his thumb actually was. He tried on the way home to get this over to his mother.

"Mammy, I thought the doctor would fix my finger. It's sore and it's throbbing a lot."

"I know, son, but the doctor knows best. We have to do as he said and get you to bed. You'll feel much better in the morning."

The boy did not think so…and he was quite right. He spent the next week in a stupor of fitful sleeping and waking pain. He moaned when awake and drifted back into the land of sleep where there were no headaches or throbbing in his thumb. When roused for food and liquids, he moaned to get back to sleep. He had no appetite for being awake or eating or drinking. He wanted to die to get rid of his body's unbearable hotness and the unrelenting pain in his hand.

After five days of this, Jeanie finally had had enough. She realised the doctor was wrong. She took her son back to see Doctor Ashby. The boy was so weak that he hardly knew where he was. Doctor Ashby stood up, turned his back to the lad, and drew the boy's bandaged hand round to his front. In this way Robert could not see the scalpel that was lying on the desk. Robert groaned in pain as the doctor gently removed the dressings on his sagging patient's swollen thumb. He was shocked to see such a mass of green pus on the finger.

"Oh, dear me. You have been in the wars, Robert. This must have been extremely sore. I'm afraid I am going to have to hurt you a little bit more to get this sorted. Are you ready, son?"

"Yes," came the faint agreement

The scalpel was used twice, very quickly, to cut a wedge out of his thumb and drain the poison. The boy screamed. Jeanie caught him as he fainted. He was laid on the couch sobbing with the pain of the scalpel and the fact of being so sorely treated by his noble friend, Doctor Ashby. While he lay there, his wound was bandaged and covered with a fingerstall, held on by strings round his wrist. Jeanie was in tears as she took the prescription from the doctor.

"This is for penicillin and sterile dressings. It will fight any further infection. You must apply the dressings morning and evening for five days and get Robert to take a tablet three times each day for five days. Keep him in bed and give him plenty to drink. I think I've got all the poison out and I've applied iodine to sterilise it all. I am so sorry to have given him such suffering."

Robert heard this, and in his head he moved the man down on his list of heroes. It was not a long list, and the doctor was not at the bottom by any means. But he was no longer near the top.

Jeanie took him home, put him to bed, and went to the chemist. On her way back she went in to Katie Ward's paper shop at the top of Raglan Street. There, she phoned the adjutant at Queen Victoria School to let him know that Robert had been ill and would not be able to attend the induction on the Monday, 27th July. Major Cowgrove advised her that it was not unusual for a boy to be late and not to worry. A new date was agreed. Robert was to be presented at the school at 2pm on Monday, 11th August. On that day he would leave Raglan Street behind…and his mother.

TEN
1953 – 59

Queen Victoria School

Although he had been given a lot of encouragement from Hetty and his mother for this major change in his life, Robert was still troubled. How would he manage when he finally arrived to take up residence at Queen Victoria School? He spent many a night in bed thinking of the problems he would face. *Ah'll not know anybody there. How will ah make pals wae people ah don't know? There's bound tae be boys there that want tae fight wae me. Ah'll tell them ah'm fae Glesga. That should be enough tae scare them. If no, then ah'll just dae what John said and knee them where it hurts. When they find out ah can fight, they'll keep away frae me. If it's like the army, there's gonny be people ordering me about. Ah'll just dae as ah'm told and then they'll not give me any bother.* These uncertainties crowded his head. He was preparing his defence mechanisms. This attitude of aggression learned in the streets, intensified his resolve to try to handle whatever problems arose. He accepted that he was going to this new school. Backing down from these challenges was not an option now. He was firmly committed. *Maybe*, he concluded, *it might not be as bad as all that.* The next six years would be spent finding out.

Induction of the 'rookie'

Fully recovered at last from his poisoned finger, Robert once again walked with Jeanie up the driveway of Queen Victoria School. It was just before 2pm on the eleventh of August, 1953. After a short wait in the front office, a soldier aged about sixty came in.

"Mrs Chessar?"

"Yes."

"Hello. I am Company Sergeant Major Jock White."

"Hello, Mr White. This is my son, Robert."

"Right, laddie, you'll be with me in 'C' Company. You will be in my charge today while we get you kitted out and billeted in your dormitory. You should come with us, Mrs Chessar, while we do the rounds of the school. Is that alright?"

"Yes. How long will this take? I've got a long journey back to Glasgow."

"You'll be away in less than two hours, Mrs Chessar. I will make sure you catch the four o'clock bus at the foot of the drive that will get you back to Glasgow by six o'clock tonight. OK?"

"Thank you, Mr White."

"Call me Jock."

"Thank you, Jock."

Robert had seen soldiers in his house but none he could
remember was like Jock White. He was a craggy old guy,
wearing trousers made of tartan. He had a khaki jacket with
brass buttons. His shirt and tie were khaki. On his head was
a black, boat-shaped hat with two ribbons hanging from the
back. On the front of the hat was a silver badge with a lion
holding two swords inside of a wreath of leaves. He had a
crown sewn on each forearm of his jacket. Robert thought,
*this looks like a man you would not say 'no' to if he told you
to do something*.

They walked at a brisk pace round to the back of the school.
At the quartermaster's store, Robert was measured for his
new school outfit. Jeanie watched in silence as he was handed
two sets of brand new clothes and other essentials: short black
trousers, long-sleeved navy-blue sweaters, khaki shirts, white
woollen vests, green hankies, green top hose stockings, red
elasticated garter flashes, green underpants, black leather
brogue shoes, rugby jersey, rugby shorts, rugby boots, gym
plimsolls, white towels, blue and white striped pyjamas,
toothbrush, toothpaste (Gibbs Dentifrice) wrapped in
cellophane paper inside a flat tin, black boot polish (Cherry
Blossom) in a flat tin, a solid-brass button stick, a tin of liquid
brass polish, a set of brushes to polish his shoes and brass
buttons, a Glengarry hat with a silver cap badge, a small flat-
leather sporran with belt and chain, a battledress khaki jacket,
a khaki Inverness-cape greatcoat and a kitbag.

Then the quartermaster told him, "Just drop your trousers,
Robert, and we'll get you fitted with your kilt."

He looked at his mother with a question on his face.
Jeanie, knowing how sensitive he was, smiled and turned

away. He then looked at Jock White with the same querulous look.

"Get your breeks down, laddie. We're not going to see anything we haven't seen before."

Robert forced a smile. "Yes, Mr White."

"Your mother calls me 'Mr White', Mr McRoberts here calls me 'Jock', but you, laddie, will call me 'Sir'. Understood?

"Yes."

"Yes what?"

Robert smiled again, this time showing pleasure from Jock's clear commands. "Yes, sir!"

"Excellent, laddie."

Jeanie smiled. *He is in good hands here with Jock White, and he's learning fast.* With a little help from his mammy, who carried his kilt and greatcoat, Robert manhandled his full kitbag up to the dormitory in 'C' Company. Jock showed him his bed halfway down the dormitory.

"Right, laddie, get out of your civilian clothes and into your new school kit. Hang your kilt and khaki jacket in your locker. This evening, after you've had your tea, we'll get your kit number stencilled on all your school stuff. You've got ten minutes to get dressed while your mother and I go and have a chat. Okay?"

"Yes, sir!"

Jock smiled. He liked the boy's show of confidence and manners. He knew that getting inducted into this school was nerve-wracking for all the new recruits, but felt that this one would cope well. Showing respect for your superior officers was a pre-requisite to good soldiering. That was the ethos of this school. Some of the older boys had authority to punish wrongdoers. With the slap of a slipper on the behind of wrongdoers, they maintained firm order and discipline. They did not have a free rein, by any means; they were always under the watchful eyes of the teachers from the Royal Army Education Corps. Retired soldiers like Jock, oversaw the running of the four companies. 'C' company was for the junior boys.

Jock took Jeanie down to his office and made a pot of tea.

"How will he find his way round, Jock?"

"Nothing to worry about, Mrs Chessar. I will assign a senior boy to keep him under his wing for a few days. There is a lot to learn in the school, but he will soon pick up all he needs to know."

"How will I say goodbye to him? I am sure he will be embarrassed if I hug him in front of any of the other boys."

"A clean break is sore, but in my experience the boys get over that a lot quicker. I guess you will not be so quick to get over parting with your boy, but I promise you one thing. You will see a big difference in him when he goes home again in a couple of months. When the time comes for you to leave,

Mrs Chessar, I think it's best just to touch his shoulder, say *goodbye,* and walk away quickly.

"I will do that, Jock. Thank you for looking after us. He's been away from home a couple of times and I don't think he will suffer too much from homesickness. He'll just get on with his new life here, making the best of it, I hope."

"I'm sure he will, Mrs Chessar. I'll see he is kept busy. From what I have seen, he will soon settle into the routine here. I think he'll be dressed in his school clothes now. Let's go up and you'll see where he'll be staying for the rest of this term."

Jeanie was impressed at how smart her boy looked in his new outfit. All his other things were neatly stored in his tall locker. The dormitory was long and narrow with beds down each side, one at each of thirty windows. Robert had packed the suitcase with his civilian kit for his mother to take away. His new kit was neatly stacked in his locker.

"How did you know where all your kit was to be arranged in your locker, laddie?"

"I looked at the other lockers, sir."

"Well, Mrs Chessar, we have a quick learner. I don't think you will have any worries about him settling in. It's gone half past three so we best get you away down to catch your bus. Come with us, laddie, and you can say cheerio to your mother."

As they went downstairs to see Jeanie off, Robert spotted other boys dressed the same as him. They smiled at him as they passed and someone said, *that's the rookie*. There were other very tall people dressed in tartan trousers and khaki jackets similar to Jock White, but much younger.

"Are they the teachers, sir?"

"No, laddie, they're the senior boys. You obey them when they give you an order. You address them as 'Monitor'."

"What's a rookie, sir"?

"The boys call you a rookie because you are a new boy. Your actual rank here is 'Private'. You'll soon get to know who's who and what's what, OK?"

"Yes, sir."

They stepped out of the side door of the school building. Jock turned to Jeanie to wish her a safe journey back to Glasgow.

"You will catch your bus in about ten minutes at the foot of the driveway, Mrs Chessar. Robert, I want you to say goodbye to your mother and let her get on her way back home."

Robert had not thought about this moment when he would part from Jeanie. He stood for a moment looking at her, but didn't know what to say. She was the same. She looked at her son as if he was someone else. She seemed to see her dead husband formed in the young boy's face. She saw his blond hair and green eyes looking like his daddy. For a fleeting moment, she felt the loss of her man again by letting her boy be taken away. She wanted to put her arms around him and hug him hard to let him know how much he meant to her. She was not able to speak.

Robert spoke. "Cheerio, Mammy."

He turned and ran down the path. He had no idea where it led except that it led him away from her and Jock White. He did not look back. No-one would see his wet eyes. He didn't see the hankie Jeanie dabbed on her eyes. Neither would he see her again until Halloween, months from now. He ran out of their sight and found himself heading for the school playing fields. He stopped on the grass wondering what to do next. This was all so strange. He had run into a place and into people he did not know.

He stiffened when about a dozen inquisitive boys about his own age surrounded him. *Maybe this is where ah'll have tae fight.* He had no need to worry; all they wanted was to find out all about the 'rookie'. Jeanie was forgotten as he tried to answer their bombardment of questions. He was quite relaxed with these boys, and chatted with them for about fifteen minutes until an older boy appeared. He had two stripes on an armband on his jersey.

"Are you Robert Chessar?"

"Yes."

"Say, *yes Corporal*!"

"Yes, Corporal!"

"Good. Remember that! I'm Corporal Rennie. C.S.M. White says I have to take charge of you for a while till you get to know what to do and where to go. OK?"

"Yes, Corporal!"

Private Chessar

Corporal Robin Rennie took his new recruit on a long tour of the buildings, pointing out the church, the hospital, the laundry, the dining room, the classrooms, some areas that were out of bounds to him, and so on. He learned all the ranks of the boys, staff, and teachers. Robin answered all of the many questions Robert asked. By the end of his tour, Robert knew where to go, when to go, what to do, and how to do it. Robin acted as mentor for a week, after which Robert had run out of questions. That was when he moved from being just a 'rookie' to his proper status of 'Private'. That is when Robin left him to his own devices.

During that week, Robert had made several new friends from his dormitory who were also in his class. Now he was better equipped to begin facing the challenges of his new school. It wasn't long before he really got to grips with the army style of school life. There was quite a bit of free time but nothing like what he was used to in Glasgow.

Each day was arranged in periods. Changeovers were announced by bugle calls. The bugle signalled 'lights out!' for bedtime at nine and 'reveille!' to get up again at seven-thirty. The bugle call for meals was a tune the boys put words to: *Come to the cookhouse door, boys. Come to the cookhouse door.* You had five minutes to get from where you were in the school and into the central hall to line up and be counted. After five minutes, the bugler sounded a 'G' note. If you were not in place by then, you got a punishment. Senior boys were promoted to different levels of authority: Lance Corporals had one stripe; Corporals had two stripes; Sergeants had three stripes; monitors had a crown on their sleeve; the senior monitor had a crown on each sleeve, and had authority over all the promoted boys in the school. These promoted boys were what the army called non-commissioned officers, or N.C.O.s for short.

All boys were given what was referred to as a 'trade'. They could be a piper, a drummer, a Highland dancer, or a musician in the military band. The Regimental Sergeant Major, R.S.M. George Lowdon, assembled all the new boys in a line, walked along and tapped each boy on the head with his swagger stick, and told him his trade. There was no choice. Robert became a Highland dancer.

Homework was every night after tea. In the classrooms, a senior boy supervised in lieu of the teachers. There was a ten-acre sports field where rugby was played in the autumn and winter terms. In the summer term, the field was given over to athletics. Challenges were issued to other schools for rugby and athletics.

There was a church service every Sunday. Kilts and battledress jackets were worn. Afterwards, the pipe band led the whole school in the march past along the front of the school where the commandant stood under the flagpole to take the salute.

Robert had thought that his new life at Q.V.S. was going to be more of a trauma compared to Raglan Street. He had missed his Glasgow pals for a while during the first few days. When he returned to Raglan Street for the Hallowe'en holiday, he tried to look them up. But he had been away too long. They had found other friends at their own new secondary schools. There was also some wariness about a twelve-year-old walking into their street dressed like a WW1 soldier…all kilt and khaki jacket, with a kitbag over his shoulder. He drew a few quizzical looks as he headed down Raglan Street. Before he reached his close, he realised he was back among the slums. His superb school was the complete opposite of these dirty buildings – the rubbish bins overflowing into the backcourts; gas lighting on the stairs; broken-down windows on the stairhead; the lack of anything that was better than the place he had left only two hours ago in Perthshire.

No harm to his mother, but he was suddenly aware that he had been living like a prince in Q.V.S. There, he had a bed of his own, new clothes, four great meals every day, beautiful playing fields, and all of the fantastic activities he was involved in that could not be replicated here in Raglan Street. He wanted to turn round and go back to his school, but he needed to continue up these stairs to see his mother again and try to feel at home. It was only a long-weekend break; he would be heading back in a few days. In a few more weeks, though, he would be home again for Christmas.

That holiday was longer, but he was paraded around his relations to show off his uniform, so it was not so bad. Aunties and uncles bombarded him with questions that he enjoyed answering. At least he was the centre of attention for a while, unlike his previous days before going to Q.V.S., when he was used to *being seen and not heard*. He could now feel proud of his unique position in the family. The only one dressed as a soldier, and he was not even twelve yet!

Robert turned twelve in January 1954. On returning to school after the holidays, Jock White promoted him to 'section leader' with authority only within the 'C' company environs. This allowed the boy to order the rest of the boys in his company to do as he bid them. The Privates went to bed at nine, but he was allowed to stay up with the seniors until ten before having to go to bed. This was a rare privilege and showed the hopes that C.S.M. White had for his 'laddie' to do well. It was not to last, however. Robert got rather big-headed, shouting orders willy-nilly, and being a real pest to the rest of the N.C.O.s. They reported this to his mentor, Jock.

When Robert appeared in Jock's office for pocket money parade one Saturday morning, Jock looked at him sternly. "What are you smiling at, laddie?"

"*I'm* not smiling, sir."

"If I say you are smiling, then you are smiling!"

"I'm *not* smiling! …Sir!"

"Now you are shouting at me, laddie. You are being insubordinate, laddie! You are not fit to be a section leader in this company. Get out of here. You are no longer a section leader!"

Robert's world had just been blown apart as if a hand grenade had been chucked at him. He left the C.S.M.'s office and sat down in the corridor with his back to the cold wall, his head in his hands looking at the floor and wishing it would open up and swallow him. How could he face the boys he had been ordering about now that he had been busted down to a Private again? He heard the comments of boys going past him. Comments expected from boys who saw a swollen-headed power-hungry martinet getting his comeuppance.

"He can't shout at us any more."

"I wouldn't like to be in his place, lining up with us at 'lights out' time, now he has to go to bed at nine just like us."

"I hope he's learned his lesson."

He sat there for a long time thinking what was the best thing to do to minimise his embarrassment in the days and weeks ahead. *I could kill myself. No. That would only give Jock White satisfaction. I thought he was my friend. Why was he so cruel? Maybe if I just carry on as a Private, like nothing has happened, he will make me up to section leader again. If anybody says anything to me, I will just ignore it. That's what I'll do.* He got up and did just that.

Jock never did promote him. He had given this boy his one chance. Jock never gave anyone a second chance. He was unaware of the important effect his demotion had on Robert. It had hurt him deeply, but forced the boy to look so critically at himself that he made a solemn personal promise. *If I ever get promoted again, I will not be big-headed and shout and bawl at the other boys. I will treat them the way Corporal Rennie treated me in my first week here, firmly but fairly.*

He was to wait a long time for that promotion. It was not long, however, before his arrogance was forgotten by the other boys. There were plenty of other things to occupy these schoolboys. Holding grudges was not one of them. That was another lesson Robert learned and he was grateful for it. This was when he had another flash of insight as to how to get through the pitfalls in this enclave of tests and challenges. This was when he started to think like his big brother, John. The best thing is to try to out-think the people in charge. *John taught me if you give people what they want, like sticks for their fires, they are happy and will respect you. What the people above me want is no cheek, plenty of smiles, obedience to commands, and to look as if I am trying my best at everything I have to do. That will be my job from now on.*

From that day on, he went about smiling at the senior boys and the teachers, opening doors for them, standing to attention and saying, *Good morning, Corporal. Good afternoon Sergeant. Good evening, Monitor. Goodnight, Sir.* This worked well. He applied the same attitude to his schoolwork, his athletics, his rugby, his homework, his duties in the dining room and the dormitory, to keep tidy and clean and cause as little trouble as possible. He was never ever late to assemble for meals or school classes or church parades. He had found his personal key to survival in the maelstrom of total absorption of this magnificently-run fortress of security and opportunity. He was what the army loved: a model soldier. An onlooker might call him a broken stallion – tamed and submissive. He was not. His finely-honed instinct for survival was in play.

Prefect Chessar

After three years, he was promoted. The school authorities discontinued the army ranks for the boys. Corporals and Sergeants became prefects. Now he had a room of his own; an eight-foot square room within his dormitory. Every year, one single prefect aged fifteen who, in the opinion of the teaching staff, showed the most satisfactory progress since joining the school, got an award. It was a medal to be worn when he was on full dress parades. His name was inscribed on a brass plate fixed to the wall of the central hall of the school. Robert was awarded this distinction in 1957. He kept his promise that, with his new powers of authority over the younger boys in the school, he dealt with mischief by giving the wrongdoers a choice of punishment. Some kids did not like to be skelped by a slipper. Others did not like to get fifty or a hundred lines. There were others who did not like either of these two. The latter were told to go round the school precincts and collect five different kinds of leaf from the trees. When they brought the leaves back, they were obliged to identify them. This took time, but the youngsters were intrigued by the oddball penalty.

"Here are the five leaves, Prefect Chessar."

"Okay. What are they?"

"An Ash, an oak, a silver birch, a chestnut, and an elder, Prefect."

"That's very good, boy."

"Is that me finished, Prefect Chessar?"

"You will be…when you put them back onto the trees you took them off."

This brought a howl of anguish. The rule of the prefect was absolute. They knew Robert only had to say, *do this!* and it was law. He was happy to get their reaction and then to tell them, "Okay, just be quiet. I was kidding. But next time, I will give you a tougher time than this. Understood?

"Yes, Prefect. Thanks, Prefect."

Happiness all round at times like that; unlike some of Robert's experiences in *his* early years. He had steered clear of bullies, knowing that one day they would eventually have to leave the school. Now he was able to practise his own brand of control and respect. His teachers did not always mirror it. In a shocking parallel event, like Mr Allen in Grove Street Primary trying to belt thirty or forty boys in the playground, a Welsh teacher tried the same at Q.V.S.

The boy bugler on duty had made a mistake about the time for tea. He blew the call and the 'G' at the same time, missing out the five-minute interval, thus making most of the schoolboys late for assembly in the central hall. This was grossly wrong, but the Welsh one-pip Second Lieutenant from the RAEC was adamant that it was not. He stopped all the late boys in the corridors leading to the central hall. He called them in one at a time and proceeded to give them the strap from his Lochghelly leather belt. This act of injustice was not noticed immediately. He was attempting to belt nearly two hundred and fifty boys for something that was not their fault. He should have been belting the duty bugler who had evidently fallen asleep at his post.

The folly was halted when a senior officer arrived and questioned him. The idiocy was stopped, but he was not given any reprimand. At least, it was not done in public. Robert was not belted. If he had been ordered to put out his hand, he was prepared to challenge the authority of this Welshman by refusing to comply. Robert's rules would apply this time. This teacher was not typical of the staff, but it was wise to be wary of people who had power to hurt you without fear of retribution.

Robert had some fun one summer morning when he demonstrated his ability to commit a mass punishment in such a way that no-one was damaged in the process. The youngsters in his dormitory were all awake in bed and talking before the bugle sounded reveille. He needed his sleep but the kids were wide-awake and chattering like sparrows. He yelled at them a number of times to be quiet, but they knew he was a softie anyway, so they continued to annoy him. It was about ten minutes to seven, the sun was up high, the crows were barking out their usual chorus of discord, and Robert had had enough.

"Right, you lot. Get up! Stand by your beds and no talking!"

They got out of bed as instructed while Robert put on his sports shorts and jersey and emerged from his room.

"Get your jammies off and into your sports shorts and plimsolls!"

There were giggling like girls wondering what new punishment Prefect Chessar was devising for their enjoyment. It was illegal in this school for someone to be out of *bed* before the bugle sounded. It was unheard of for anyone to be outside the *building*. It was criminally insane for a *whole dormitory* of boys to be outside before reveille. So, as they donned their rugby shorts, they must all have been thinking, *what is he going to do?*

"Now, you lot. I don't want anyone to talk. Make your way out the back doors and down the back stairs into the small square."

They did as instructed and assembled outside the door.

"Now, walk down to the playing field without any noise."

They formed a line through habit from their drill instruction, and single-filed their way down the path onto the grass beside the pipe-band hut.

"Okay. You are going on a cross-country run round the field. Go left all the way round, up the path, up the back stairs. Get your pyjamas on and into your beds. Last one in bed gets the slipper. Ready! Steady! Go!"

The perimeter of the field was about three-quarters of a mile. If you happened to be driving northwards on the Perth Road at seven o'clock that morning, next to the playing fields of Q.V.S., you would have seen a stream of ten-year-olds running round the edges of the huge expanse of grass. You may have thought how cruel it was to treat boys like that. You would have been wrong. The children loved it. It was different. They revelled in doing something dangerously idiotic; especially since it would be Prefect Chessar who would get it in the neck if they were seen. Prefect Chessar knew that they were seen. He saw teachers looking out from their windows in the married quarters. They could not miss this unique episode.

The scene in the dormitory was hilarious. Thirty boys were at various stages struggling out of their sweaty running gear, pulling on their pyjamas, and getting under the covers just as the bugler sounded the morning call to get up. There was uproar. They cheered and laughed and chattered happily as they returned to their well-practised routine of getting washed, dressed, and ready to go down for breakfast. Robert declared a 'dead heat' so no-one got the slipper.

He was not challenged for his gross disrespect of school rules. The teacher in charge at the dining hall that morning was the sports master. He whispered a comment in Robert's ear.

"Nice one, Chess. Good for their morale, but I wouldn't do it again."

"I'm sure I have no idea what you're talking about, sir?"

"Sorry, Chess, it must have been someone else, eh?"

"I'm sure you are correct, sir."

This was an example of the mutual respect between the senior boys and some of the more enlightened staff and teachers. After all, many of these boys were young men in the making; virtually adults. They shaved, their voices were deepening, and sometimes the younger teachers joined in with them on the rugby field. That was when the staff found that they were not invincible, and the boys began to realise their *own* potential.

This period of Robert's stay at the school showed he had more in him than he had thought possible. He was beginning to believe that there was a better future than had he gone to secondary school in Glasgow. He was in a class of eight bright pupils in sixth year. He had achieved so many things that would not have been available in Glasgow. He was a champion Highland dancer. He had performed in the Tattoo in Edinburgh Castle for a month the summer after he joined the school. He had been trained to fire small bore 0.22 rifles, 0.45 semi-automatic pistols, 0.45 Sten guns, .303 Lee Enfield rifles, and Light Machine Guns (Bren Guns). He could strip and re-assemble a Bren gun in 32 seconds blindfolded. He was the school high jump champion, and won the 1958 National Army Cadet Force (A.C.F.) championship in London, and out-jumped all the private schools in Perthshire.

He had taken a platoon of cadets in rowing boats across the sea from Oban to the island of Kerrera and stayed under canvas for two nights without being detected. He had learned to drive a British Army 'Champ' jeep with a Rolls Royce engine. Had spent a summer holiday supervising the junior school on a tented camping trip to the peninsula on Loch Awe that held the ruins of Kilchurn Castle, an ancient stronghold of Clan Campbell (Robert's middle name). He played in the school first fifteen rugby team as a prop forward, and scored his one and only try during a game with Fettes College in Edinburgh.

He was given a present of a new bicycle by his mother on becoming a prefect, and used it on three occasions to visit her by cycling from school to Raglan Street and back again the same day. He was a fully competent drill instructor for the privates learning to march. He was the colour sergeant on school parades. He was batman to the school padre. He took part in the school variety comedy shows, and produced one himself that went down well with the whole school and staff in attendance. He gained valuable qualifications, giving him the confidence to seek a career as a draughtsman. He had no desire to join the military, even although the six years of training in Q.V.S. was certain to ensure an easy entry to any chosen branch of the services. Raglan Street was coming second by a long way in his life.

Going Home

It was always a problem for Robert to leave for holidays and return to Raglan Street. It got harder to do this the older he got. His friends who lived in Glasgow came from smarter parts of the town. Their houses were much bigger. These boys had no problem leaving the school, because they never felt their homes to be inferior to Q.V.S. Some had fathers who were officers in the services. Robert was embarrassed by his humble tenement house, and would not invite his Q.V.S. pals to visit him at home. These feelings hurt him sorely every time he went home. He was paranoid about not letting anyone know how poor, in his opinion, his life was at home. He was not at all proud of his humble beginnings, and had been successful in disguising it from his friends at school.

The problem was that he could not disguise it from himself; it haunted him every time he went home. There was no escape from his distress. He had no means of solving this problem. It was not of his making. It was the damned war that had taken away his father, leaving his mother and his family practically destitute. There was simply not enough money to get out of the slums. Was he going to have to stay here forever? His only hope of getting out of it was to get a job that paid enough money, but that was going to take years and years and years. The one thing that sustained him through his trauma was going back to his beautiful Q.V.S. There he had his own bed in his own room and all the fabulous facilities of the place at his disposal. He was well respected by his peers and the teaching staff. Life was very sweet during his final years in this grand place. He had status and comfort, but all good things must come to an end!

In August 1959, six years exactly since he joined his boarding school, Robert left for the last time and returned to his tenement at 27 Raglan Street. There was now no going back. Q.V.S. was over!

New career

It was time to find a job. His search began with visits to Glasgow's main engineering works and shipyards, looking to train as a draughtsman. None of these offered him a job. After a week of perseverance, he got an interview with an engineering firm whose offices were not far from Raglan Street. The manager was an ex-RAF Flight Lieutenant who seemed impressed by the boy's military school background. Robert was careful to speak confidently but avoid seeming cocky. The sore lesson from Jock White was ingrained in him. The interview was short and pleasant. He was given the position as the junior of five indentured apprentice draughtsmen.

From being a bigwig in his school, Robert was a 'rookie' again! His Q.V.S. survival tactics would stand him in good stead: *keep your head down, work hard, obey orders, and be the best that you can be.* In five years he would become a fully qualified journeyman and start to earn a good salary. It would take its time, but he was determined to stick it out and gain promotion. All he needed now was to get out of the slums.

He was patient. Like his wishes for a bike, a daddy, and a fur coat for his mother, he would keep wishing for better. *One day,* he thought. *One day I will get out and have somewhere better to live.*

Two years later, he was delighted to learn that his house at 27 Raglan Street was to be demolished.

-

EPILOGUE

In 1962, standing at the back close and still here to tell the tale, Robert never dreamed that so many memories would remain so clear inside the head of a one-time ragamuffin from 27 Raglan Street, Glasgow, G4.

But they did.

And there are *many* more.

Before Robert was born, Lion Street was separated from Raglan Street's backcourts by a long high brick wall, middens, and washhouses. The Lion Street tenements were removed when Robert was nearing nine years of age. The Lion Street folk were relocated under the slum clearances programme long before Raglan Street was demolished. Just before the actual demolitions began, the kids from Raglan Street explored the empty buildings. Such incursion into the territory of their one-time enemies was probably the first time they had even ventured over the wall, never mind entered any of the houses. Raglan Street was bad enough for social deprivation, but Lion Street was considerably worse off. In the First World War, all the men in Lion Street joined up as a group of friends to fight for 'King and Country'. They were all wiped out, leaving the women back home to suffer grinding poverty. It is small wonder that the people from that street were tough.

One of the houses was not yet emptied of its furniture and contents. It was into this that Robert ventured with his pals. It had been the home of some old person who had either died or had just gone away to doss down in some other part of the town, rather than be re-housed far away. The furniture was old and smelly. A chest of drawers was full of old clothes, and the kitchen was piled with unwashed dishes and mouldy old milk bottles.

There were the usual accoutrements and utensils required for cooking and eating, but everything was worn out and dirty. The floorboards were caked with spilled food and liquids. Poking around in this person's home made Robert feel like an intruder on some old person's privacy. In a typical display of concern for the missing or dead old buddy, the boys agreed they should leave everything as they had found it, and went out without stealing anything or causing any damage.

It was not long before the bulldozers came and tore the buildings down. For about two weeks, the people of Raglan Street, facing Lion Street, had to put up with the dirt and dust of the demolition, the smoke of the fires burning all of the recovered timbers from that street, and the migration of the newly homeless rats and mice. It was an exciting time for the children to see such huge devastation literally in their own backyard. When it was all eventually cleared, it left a big open playground for them.

As the next years went by, the wall between the two areas gradually, brick by reluctant brick, disappeared by the action of the kids. Then it was possible to take a short cut from Raglan Street through Lion Street and into town, via

Garscube Road. This was one of the places where pitch and toss gamblers met. Sundays brought out the street football teams, providing free entertainment. The area remained in this state for almost twelve years until Robert's side of Raglan Street was taken away in 1962 to make way for a new primary school.

The bulldozers moved in after that to clear away the rest of Raglan Street, Braco Street, St George's Road, North Woodside Road, Westbury Street, Cedar Street, Balnain Street, Grove Street, St Peter's Street, Braid Street, Lilac Place, Windsor Terrace, and whole swathes of other streets around the area of Cowcaddens and Woodside.

This took away the houses of Robert's grandmother, Aunt May, Aunt Maggie, and Aunt Lizzie, the primary school he attended as a youngster, the shops where he hired bicycles, the pubs where he sold back his empty bottles, the cinemas he went to with his big brother John for the Saturday matinees, the grocer's, the dairy, the newspaper shop, the fishmonger's, the toy shop, the chip shop, Ram Singh's bike hire shop, the chemist's shop, the barber's shop, the baker's shop, Mary Began's sweet shop, and all of the exciting and magical places where he had experienced all of the adventures related here, and more that remain to be told.

In the later redevelopment of the area, the Co-operative furniture store was taken down at St George's Cross. Credit must be given to some far-sited architect for saving the statue of *St George and the Dragon* that sat high up on its roof. Nostalgic folk can look at it on its ground-level plinth on the island at St George's Cross.

The Empress Theatre, later called *The Metropole* by its new owner, Jimmy Logan – and the place of Robert's earliest awakening to the mysteries of life – was removed to accommodate some modern flats, which no doubt bring in much more revenue than the old theatre did in its time. Perhaps not the same joys inside...or out?

On returning to the scenes of his childhood, the author is torn between the strength of his yearning for things now gone, and his conviction that he would not wish his kind of childhood on modern kids. The latter is out of the question because, by comparison with yesteryear, the last sixty years of 'improvement' in the places of his childhood are disappointing and technology has changed the world of play for young ones of today.

Some people reading this may ask themselves if they would give up what today's world has to offer and return to the harsh and challenging conditions of their childhood. Their parents had to raise them through real poverty and austerity, with a little dignity, trying to engender some sense of worth they could take into the future. Could this generation take that on today? Robert is proud and glad, however, that he had a family that did just that for him. He is proud now of those humble beginnings and grateful for the opportunity to articulate these snapshots of his early life. The images in this tale will hopefully appeal to his fellow travellers from that time – Bertie, John, Ian, Archie, and others from the surrounding streets.

What if all of us ex-street urchins could see a gang of today's kids rolling rubber tyres to Milngavie and spending the day playing on a riverbed with no money and only themselves to amuse?

Just for absolute clarity to finish off this yarn, Jeanie eventually bought herself a Beaver Lamb fur coat, which, after all these years, the author still has in his wardrobe at home. She also bought two bicycles: one for John, and one for his wee brother. She never re-married, so the boys never had a father. In hindsight, they never really needed one...not with wee Jeanie in charge.

Bob Chessar. Born 16th January, 1942